Assessment of Nonpoint Source Chemical Loading Potential to Watersheds Containing Uranium Waste Dumps and Human Health Hazards Associated with Uranium Exploration and Mining, Red, White, and Fry Canyons, Southeastern Utah, 2007

By Kimberly R. Beisner, Thomas M. Marston, and David L. Naftz, U.S. Geological Survey, Terry Snyder, Bureau of Land Management, and Michael L. Freeman, U.S. Geological Survey

Prepared in cooperation with the Bureau of Land Management

Scientific Investigations Report 2010–5108

U.S. Department of the Interior
U.S. Geological Survey

U.S. Department of the Interior
KEN SALAZAR, Secretary

U.S. Geological Survey
Marcia K. McNutt, Director

U.S. Geological Survey, Reston, Virginia: 2010

For more information on the USGS—the Federal source for science about the Earth, its natural and living resources, natural hazards, and the environment, visit http://www.usgs.gov or call 1-888-ASK-USGS

For an overview of USGS information products, including maps, imagery, and publications, visit http://www.usgs.gov/pubprod

To order this and other USGS information products, visit http://store.usgs.gov

Suggested citation:
Beisner, K.R., Marston, T.M., Naftz, D.L., Snyder, Terry, and Freeman, M.L., 2010, Assessment of nonpoint source chemical loading potential to watersheds containing uranium waste dumps and human health hazards associated with uranium exploration and mining, Red, White, and Fry Canyons, southeastern Utah, 2007: U.S. Geological Survey Scientific Investigations Report 2010-5108, 30 p.

Contents

Figures

Tables

Conversion Factors, Datums, and Abbreviated Water-Quality Units

Multiply	By	To obtain
Length		
centimeter (cm)	0.3937	inch (in.)
meter (m)	3.281	foot (ft)
kilometer (km)	0.6214	mile (mi)
Area		
square kilometer (km^2)	0.3861	square mile (mi^2)
Volume		
liter (L)	33.82	ounce, fluid (fl. oz)
liter (L)	0.264	gallons (gal)
Mass		
gram (g)	0.03527	ounce, avoirdupois (oz)
Volumetric Flow Rate		
cubic meter per second (m^3/s)	35.314454	cubic feet per second (cfs)
Concentration		
milligram per liter (mg/L)	1	parts per million (ppm)
microgram per liter (µg/L)	1	parts per billion (ppb)
milligram per kilogram (mg/kg)	1	parts per million (ppm)
Radiation Dosage		
sievert (Sv)	100,000	millirem (mrem)

Temperature in degrees Celsius (°C) may be converted to degrees Fahrenheit (°F) as follows:

°F = (1.8 × °C) + 32.

Vertical coordinate information is referenced to the North American Vertical Datum of 1988 (NAVD 88).

Horizontal coordinate information is referenced to the North American Datum of 1983 (NAD 83).

Altitude, as used in this report, refers to distance above the vertical datum.

Specific conductance is given in microsiemens per centimeter at 25 degrees Celsius (µS/cm at 25°C).

Concentrations of chemical constituents in water are given either in milligrams per liter (mg/L) or micrograms per liter (µg/L).

Abbreviated Water-Quality Units

Major constituent	Abbreviation
Alkalinity	$CaCO_3$
Calcium	Ca
Magnesium	Mg
Potassium	K
Sodium	Na
Sulfate	SO_4

Trace element	Abbreviation
Aluminum	Al
Antimony	Sb
Arsenic	As
Barium	Ba
Beryllium	Be
Cadmium	Cd
Chromium	Cr
Cobalt	Co
Copper	Cu
Iron	Fe
Lead	Pb
Manganese	Mn
Molybdenum	Mo
Nickel	Ni
Selenium	Se
Silver	Ag
Thallium	Tl
Uranium	U
Vanadium	V
Zinc	Zn

Assessment of Nonpoint Source Chemical Loading Potential to Watersheds Containing Uranium Waste Dumps and Human Health Hazards Associated with Uranium Exploration and Mining, Red, White, and Fry Canyons, Southeastern Utah, 2007

By Kimberly R. Beisner, Thomas M. Marston, and David L. Naftz, U.S. Geological Survey, Terry Snyder, Bureau of Land Management, and Michael L. Freeman, U.S. Geological Survey

Abstract

During May, June, and July 2007, 58 solid-phase samples were collected from abandoned uranium mine waste dumps, background sites, and adjacent streambeds in Red, White, and Fry Canyons in southeastern Utah. The objectives of this sampling program were to (1) assess the nonpoint-source chemical loading potential to ephemeral and perennial drainage basins from uranium waste dumps and (2) assess potential effects on human health due to recreational activities on and around uranium waste dumps on Bureau of Land Management property. Uranium waste-dump samples were collected using solid-phase sampling protocols. After collection, solid-phase samples were homogenized and extracted in the laboratory using a leaching procedure. Filtered (0.45 micron) water samples were obtained from the field leaching procedure and were analyzed for major and trace elements at the Inductively Coupled Plasma-Mass Spectrometry Metals Analysis Laboratory at the University of Utah. A subset of the solid-phase samples also were digested with strong acids and analyzed for major ions and trace elements at the U.S. Geological Survey Geologic Division Laboratory in Denver, Colorado.

For the initial ranking of chemical loading potential for uranium waste dumps, results of leachate analyses were compared with existing aquatic-life and drinking-water-quality standards. To assess potential effects on human health, solid-phase digestion values for uranium were compared to soil screening levels (SSL) computed using the computer model RESRAD 6.5 for a probable concentration of radium. One or more chemical constituents exceeded aquatic life and drinking-water-quality standards in approximately 64 percent (29/45) of the leachate samples extracted from uranium waste dumps. Most of the uranium waste dump sites with elevated

trace-element concentrations in leachates were located in Red Canyon. Approximately 69 percent (31/45) of the strong acid digestible soil concentration values were greater than a calculated SSL. Uranium waste dump sites with elevated leachate and total digestible concentrations may need to be further investigated to determine the most appropriate remediation method.

Introduction

Red, White, and Fry Canyons in San Juan County, Utah, in the Colorado Plateau physiographic province encompass approximately 400 mi^2 of primarily Bureau of Land Management (BLM) property (fig. 1). Red, White, and Fry Canyons generally are linear with a drainage direction toward the northwest and altitudes ranging from 3,700 to 7,500 ft. Exposed rocks range in age from the Permian (Cutler Formation) through the Jurassic (Navajo Sandstone). Most of the land is covered by ephemeral streams that only contribute runoff during rainfall and snowmelt events. Red Canyon and a smaller canyon, Blue Notch Canyon, drain into Good Hope Bay on Lake Powell. Fry Canyon drains into White Canyon, which enters Lake Powell north of Good Hope Bay.

Red, White, and Fry Canyons are characterized by mild winters and hot summers. Most of the precipitation falls as rain from convective thunderstorms that typically occur between August and October. This arid region receives approximately 6 to 8 in. of precipitation at the lower altitudes and approximately 8 to 10 in. of precipitation at the higher altitudes (Natural Resources Conservation Service, 1998).

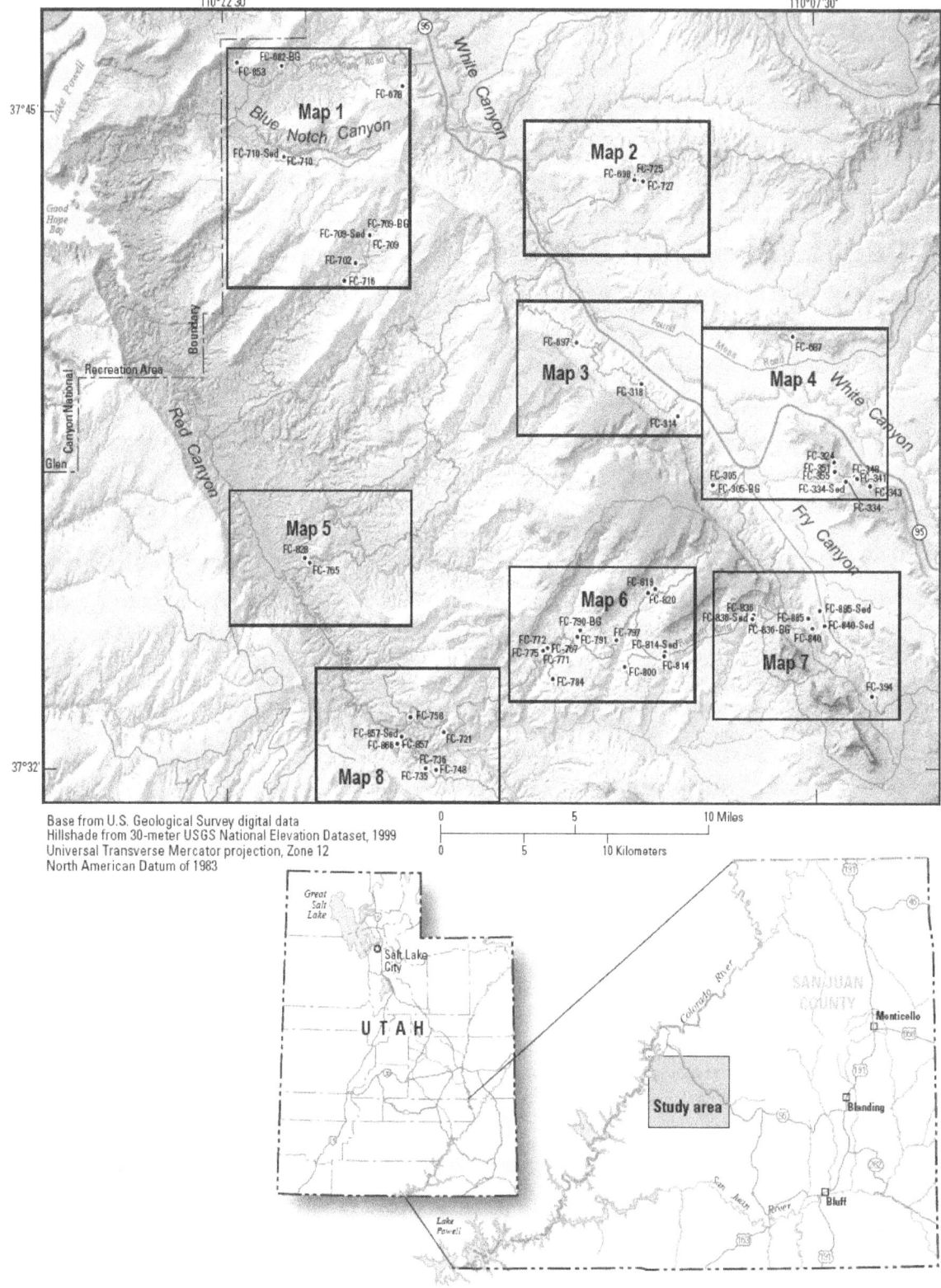

Figure 1.   Areas where uranium waste dumps, streambed sediment, and background sites were sampled, southeastern Utah.

Several areas in southern Utah experienced an increase in uranium mining and exploration in the 1950s. Most of the mines extracted uranium ore from the Triassic Chinle Formation, which is overlain by the Wingate Sandstone and is underlain by the Moenkopi Formation. At the time of publication, thousands of abandoned uranium mine waste dumps exist throughout the State of Utah, with many of the properties located on lands managed by the BLM. Approximately 65 uranium waste dump sites and adits have been inventoried by the BLM throughout Red, White, and Fry Canyons (Terry Snyder, Bureau of Land Management, written commun., 2007); however, several of those mines were not accessible during this study so only 45 abandoned uranium mines with waste dumps were sampled for this study (table 1). These abandoned uranium mine waste dumps have unique characteristics that make it difficult to quantify nonpoint source pollution contributions to specific watersheds. These characteristics include (1) locations that are primarily in watersheds with ephemeral streams, (2) radioactive sands and fine particulates that are radioactive for hundreds of thousands of years, (3) intense rainfall and snowmelt events that can

mobilize and transport mine waste with associated radioactive material and trace elements long distances during relatively short periods, and (4) remote locations that do not allow for cost effective water and suspended-sediment sampling during storm and snowmelt runoff events.

Sample collection from uranium waste dump sites during May, June, and July 2007 was completed by the U.S. Geological Survey (USGS) in cooperation with the BLM. The objectives of this sampling program were to (1) assess the nonpoint source chemical loading potential to ephemeral and perennial watersheds from uranium waste dumps and (2) assess potential impacts on human health due to recreational activities on and around uranium waste dumps on Bureau of Land Management property. Initial ranking of the chemical loading potential of each sample was done by comparing the leachate composition with existing U.S. Environmental Protection Agency (USEPA) water-quality standards for drinking water and aquatic life. Solid-phase acid extractable results were compared to soil screening levels using USEPA factors for carcinogenic effects to human health.

Table 1. U.S. Geological Survey site identification and associated Bureau of Land Management tag numbers for abandoned uranium mines with waste dumps, Red, White, and Fry Canyons, southeastern Utah.

[USGS Site ID, U.S. Geological Survey Site Identification; BLM, Bureau of Land Management; FC, Fry Canyon area]

USGS Site ID	BLM Tag Number	USGS Site ID	BLM Tag Number
FC-305	UT67800110 and UT67800123	FC-736	UT67800085
FC-314	UT67800126	FC-748	UT67800087
FC-318	UT67800127	FC-758	UT67800088
FC-324	UT67800117	FC-765	UT67800090
FC-334	UT67800119	FC-767	UT67800091
FC-341	UT67800119	FC-771	UT67800091
FC-343	UT67800124	FC-772	UT67800091
FC-348	UT67800119	FC-775	UT67800091
FC-351	UT67800116	FC-784	UT67800092
FC-355	UT67800118	FC-791	UT67800094
FC-394	UT67800125	FC-797	UT67800095
FC-678	UT67800065	FC-800	UT67800096
FC-687	UT67800069	FC-814	UT67800099
FC-697	UT67800071	FC-819	UT67800100
FC-698	UT67800072	FC-820	UT67800101
FC-702	UT67800076	FC-828	UT67800102
FC-709	UT67800076	FC-836	UT67800106
FC-710	UT67800077	FC-840	UT67800107
FC-716	UT67800078	FC-853	UT67800114
FC-721	UT67800079	FC-857	UT67800121
FC-725	UT67800082	FC-866	UT67800121
FC-727	UT67800083	FC-885	UT67800108
FC-735	UT67800085		

Methodology

Solid-Phase Sample Collection

Fifty-eight samples from 45 uranium waste dump sites, 8 streambed-sediment sites, and 5 background sites were collected in May, June, and July 2007, using a modified version of the solid-phase sampling methods outlined by Smith and others (2000) and Hageman and Briggs (2000). The general locations of uranium waste dump, background, and streambed-sediment sites that were sampled are shown in figure 1, and more detailed maps of the sampled sites are shown in figures 2–9. Because of the steep embankments of the uranium waste dumps, sampling generally took place from the safest and most accessible location. A few of the BLM inventoried sites that were unsafe to access were not sampled. Background samples were collected in the same geologic layer adjacent to sampled uranium waste dump sites. Approximately one background sample was collected for every 10 uranium waste dump samples to collect a representative selection of background samples. Streambed sediment samples were collected from ephemeral stream channels downstream from sampled uranium waste dump sites.

Samples from uranium waste dump and geologic background sites consisted of 30 scoops of soil collected from as deep as 15 cm using a plastic trowel. Scoops of soil were combined into 5-gallon plastic buckets, sealed with lids, and labeled. Streambed-sediment samples were collected along ephemeral stream channels using a plastic trowel, and these samples consisted of 10 scoops from as deep as 15 cm. Each streambed scoop location was chosen at random from a 10- to 30-m transect across the channel downstream of a sampled uranium waste dump site. Scoops of sediment were compiled into 1-gallon plastic Ziploc® bags and labeled.

Uranium waste dump sites were labeled FC (Fry Canyon) and background sites were given the same number as the associated uranium waste dump and were labeled FC-BG (Fry Canyon-Background). Streambed-sediment samples were labeled FC-SED (Fry Canyon-Sediment). Fry Canyon sample IDs that were assigned to the abandoned uranium mines by the USGS have been paired with the site IDs assigned by the BLM and are shown in table 1.

All sampling equipment was thoroughly cleaned in the field between each sampling location. An all-plastic multi-purpose sprayer was used to wash plastic trowels, collection buckets, and lids. Each item was rinsed three times with de-ionized water, wiped with a clean towel, and allowed to air dry before use at the next site.

Field Leachate Extraction Procedure

In September 2007, after the collection of solid-phase samples, aqueous phase leachate samples were extracted in the laboratory using a field-leaching procedure. Solid-phase samples were thoroughly mixed using a plastic trowel, after which approximately 800 g of sediment were measured using a pan balance, transferred to a 1-L glass beaker, and allowed to air dry. The dried sample was then sieved through a 2-mm stainless-steel mesh screen.

Fifty grams of sieved sample were added to 1,000 g of deionized water to create a 1:20 solid-to-liquid ratio. The sieved sample and water were then mixed in a precleaned 1.5-L wide-mouth high-density polyethylene (HDPE) Nalgene® bottle and agitated for 5 minutes on a shaker table operating at 170 oscillations per minute. After shaking, the samples were allowed to settle for 1 hour prior to filtration.

The leachate water was filtered through a 0.45-micron high-capacity Versapor® membrane capsule filter (GeoTech dispos-a-filter™) using precleaned tubing and a peristaltic pump. For each leachate sample, the filtered water samples were collected in one 125-mL HDPE bottle and one 125-mL acid-rinsed HDPE bottle. The samples collected in the 125-mL HDPE bottles were sent to the USGS National Water Quality Laboratory (NWQL) in Denver, Colorado, for SO_4 and alkalinity analysis. The samples collected in 125-mL acid-rinsed HDPE bottles were preserved with 1-mL Ultrex-grade 7.7N nitric acid and sent to the Inductively Coupled Plasma-Mass Spectrometry (ICP-MS) Metals Analysis Laboratory at the University of Utah for major-ion and trace-element analysis (Ag, Al, As, Ba, Be, Ca, Cd, Co, Cr, Cu, Fe, K, Mg, Mn, Mo, Na, Ni, Pb, Sb, Se, Tl, U, V, and Zn). The remaining unfiltered aliquot of water was then decanted and used to measure specific conductance and pH.

Bottles and tubing used for sample extraction were cleaned according to the USGS inorganic constituents cleaning procedures outlined in Wilde (2004). One process blank and one replicate sample were processed after every 10 leachate samples. All process blank samples were labeled as FC BLANK and given an individual extraction time and date. Blanks and replicates were analyzed at the ICP-MS Metals Analysis Laboratory at the University of Utah and the USGS NWQL. Process blank samples followed the same extraction procedures as leachate samples in the laboratory, but process blank samples were agitated without any sediment in the 1.5-L Nalgene® bottles.

Results of chemical analysis for the five process blank samples are presented in table 2. Most of the trace-element concentrations for the process blank samples were less than the lower reporting limits; however, concentrations for Ag, Cd, Co, Cr, Cu, Fe, Mn, Mo, and Sb exceeded the lower reporting limits. All Ag concentrations were equal to or less than the lower reporting limit with the exception of one blank sample (0.008 µg/L). All Cd concentrations were equal to or less than the lower reporting limit with the exception of one blank sample (0.04 µg/L). Concentrations of Co ranged from 0.11 to 0.26 µg/L with a median concentration of 0.18 µg/L. All Cr concentrations were less than the lower reporting limit with the exception of one blank sample (0.06 µg/L). All Cu concentrations were less than the lower reporting limit with the exception of one blank sample (0.98 µg/L). All Fe concentrations were less than the lower reporting limit with the

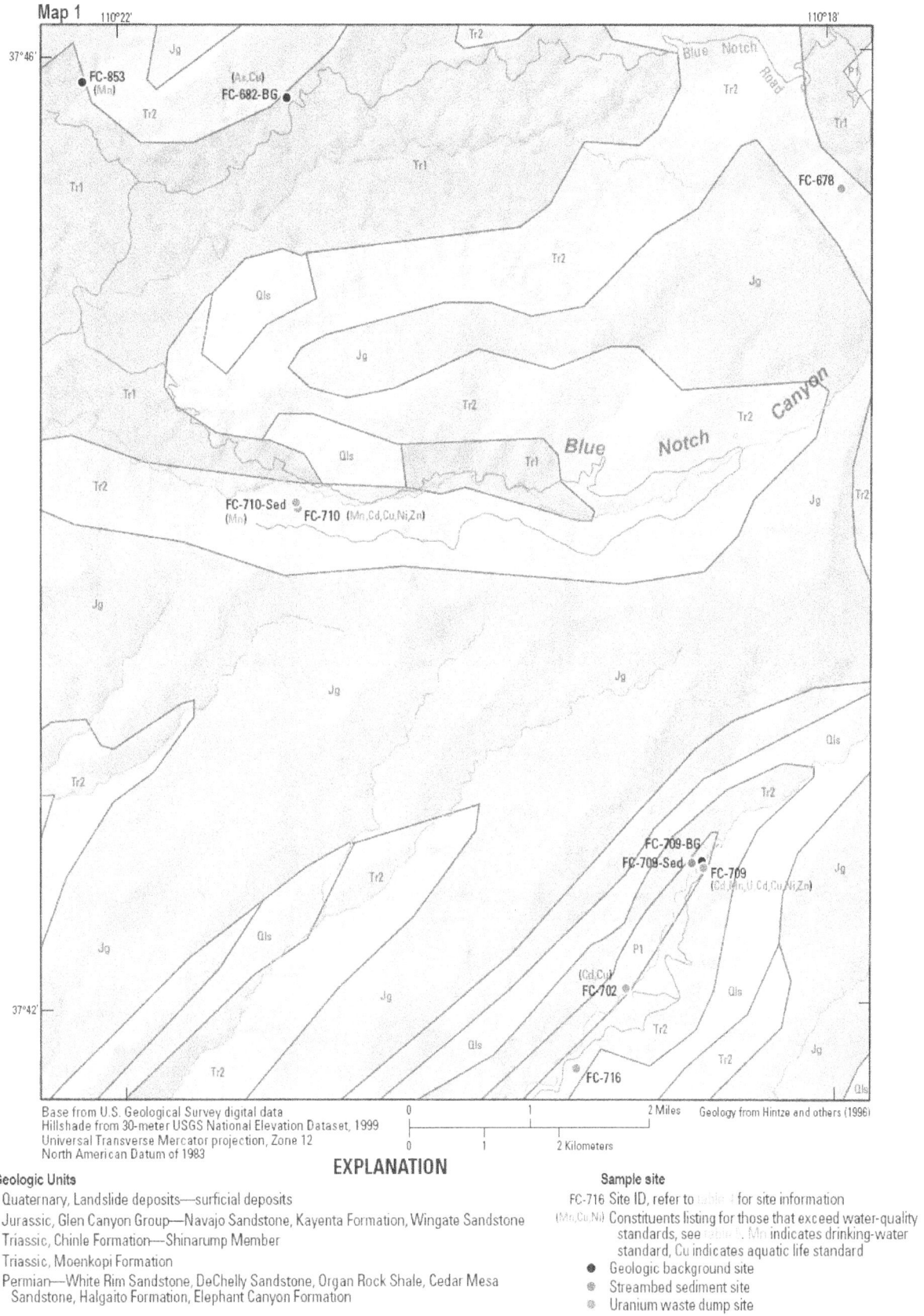

Figure 2.   Location of uranium waste dump, streambed sediment, and background sites in Map 1 where solid-phase material was collected.

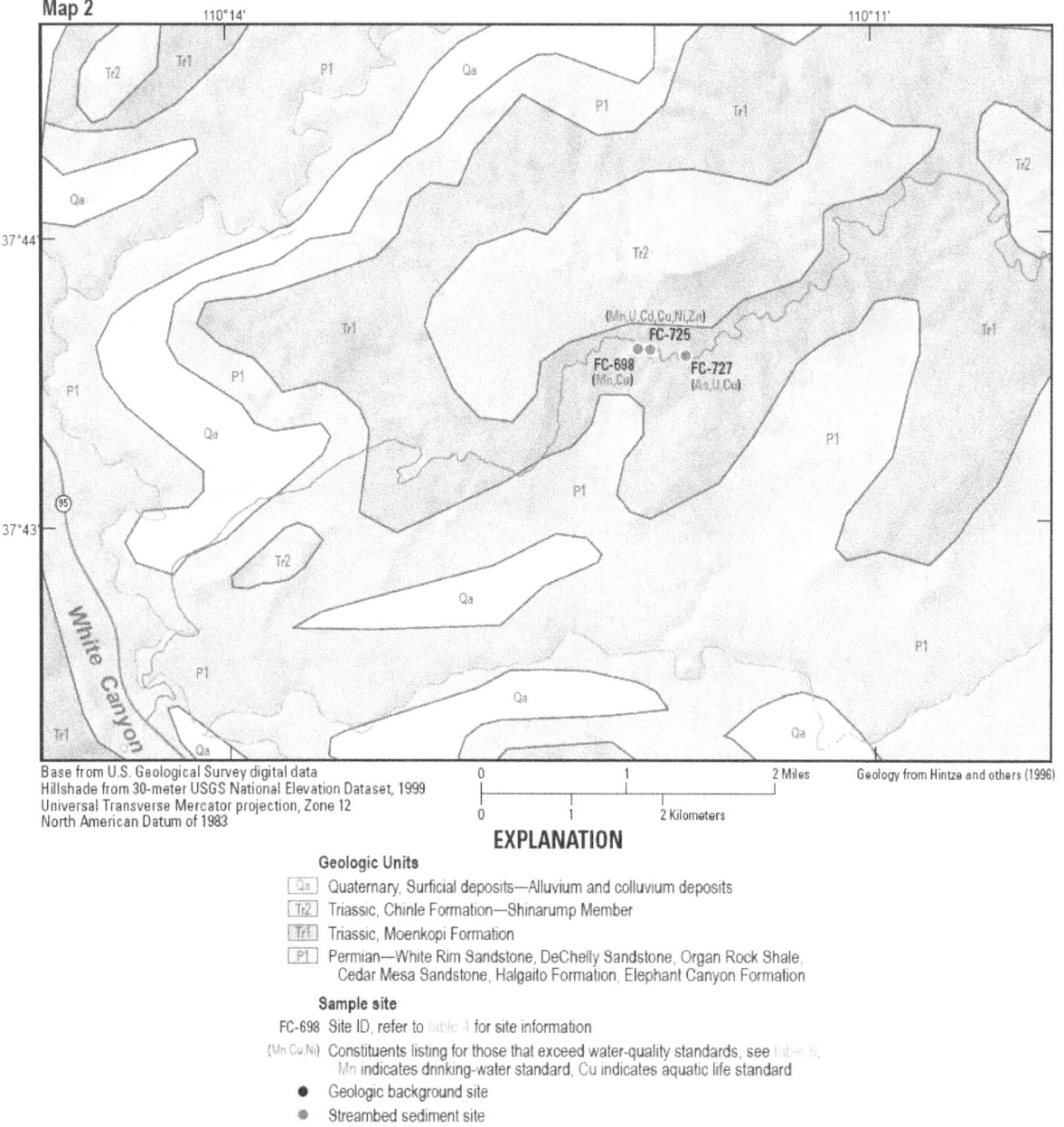

EXPLANATION

Geologic Units

Qa Quaternary, Surficial deposits—Alluvium and colluvium deposits

Tr2 Triassic, Chinle Formation—Shinarump Member

Tr1 Triassic, Moenkopi Formation

P1 Permian—White Rim Sandstone, DeChelly Sandstone, Organ Rock Shale, Cedar Mesa Sandstone, Halgaito Formation, Elephant Canyon Formation

Sample site

FC-698 Site ID, refer to Table 4 for site information

(Mn,Cu,Ni) Constituents listing for those that exceed water-quality standards, see Table 5. Mn indicates drinking-water standard, Cu indicates aquatic life standard

● Geologic background site

● Streambed sediment site

● Uranium waste dump site

Figure 3.   Location of uranium waste dump, streambed sediment, and background sites in Map 2 where solid-phase material was collected.

Map 3

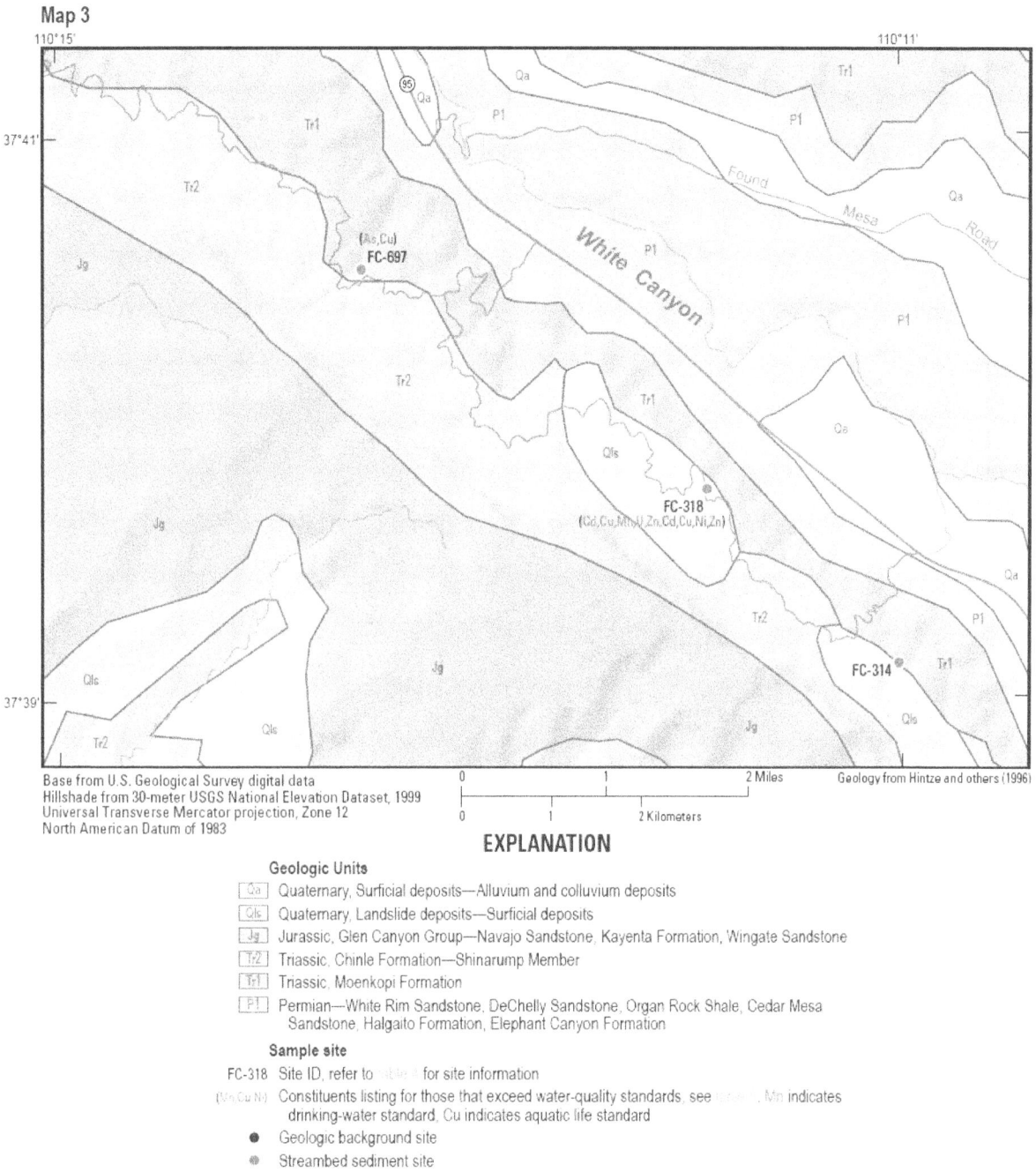

Base from U.S. Geological Survey digital data
Hillshade from 30-meter USGS National Elevation Dataset, 1999
Universal Transverse Mercator projection, Zone 12
North American Datum of 1983

Geology from Hintze and others (1996)

0   1   2 Miles

0   1   2 Kilometers

EXPLANATION

Geologic Units

Qa   Quaternary, Surficial deposits—Alluvium and colluvium deposits

Qls   Quaternary, Landslide deposits—Surficial deposits

Jg   Jurassic, Glen Canyon Group—Navajo Sandstone, Kayenta Formation, Wingate Sandstone

Tr2   Triassic, Chinle Formation—Shinarump Member

Tr1   Triassic, Moenkopi Formation

P1   Permian—White Rim Sandstone, DeChelly Sandstone, Organ Rock Shale, Cedar Mesa
       Sandstone, Halgaito Formation, Elephant Canyon Formation

Sample site

FC-318   Site ID, refer to   for site information

(Mn,Cu,Ni)   Constituents listing for those that exceed water-quality standards, see   , Mn indicates
              drinking-water standard, Cu indicates aquatic life standard

●   Geologic background site

◉   Streambed sediment site

◉   Uranium waste dump site

Figure 4.   Location of uranium waste dump, streambed sediment, and background sites in Map 3 where solid-phase material was
collected.

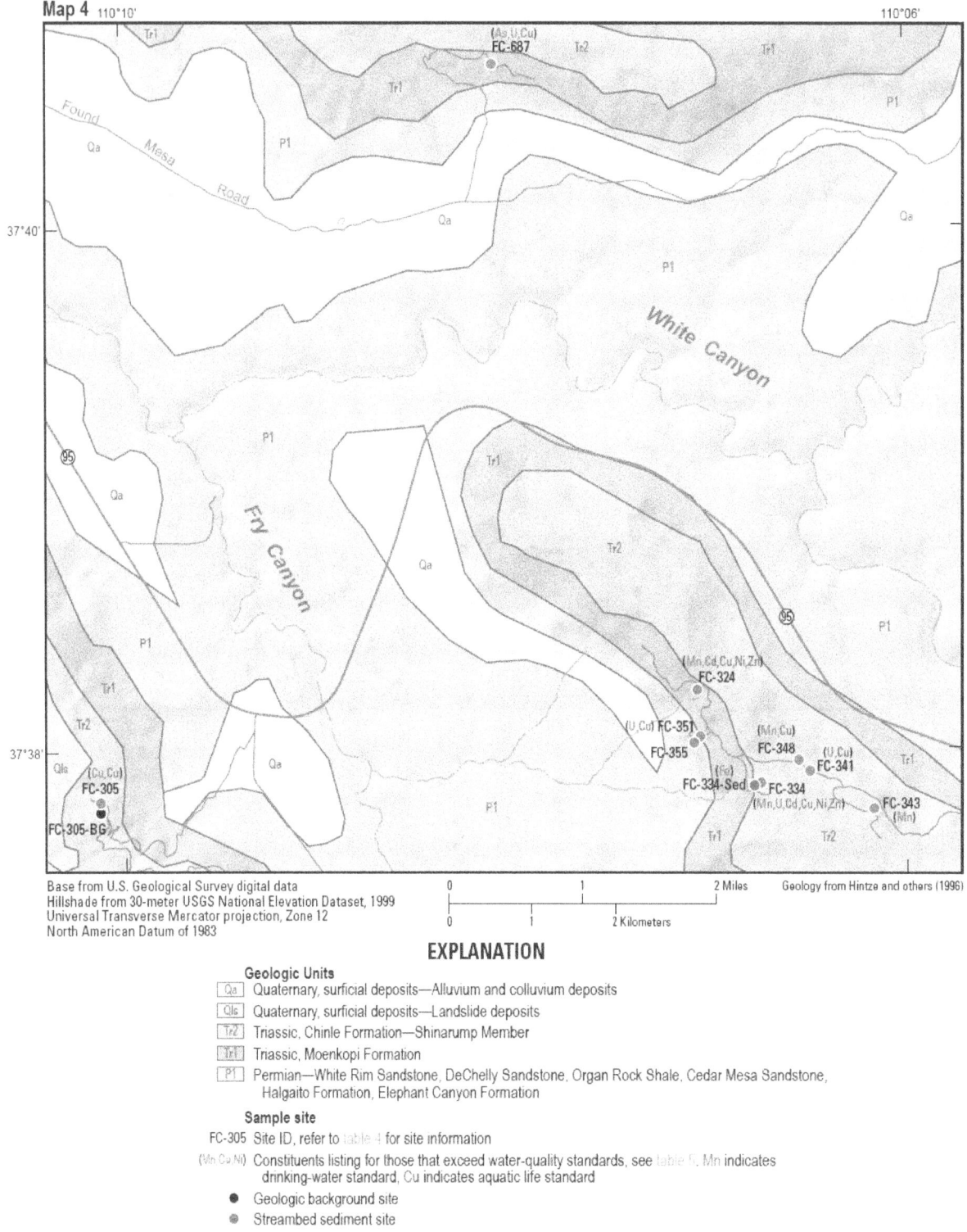

Base from U.S. Geological Survey digital data
Hillshade from 30-meter USGS National Elevation Dataset, 1999
Universal Transverse Mercator projection, Zone 12
North American Datum of 1983

Geology from Hintze and others (1996)

EXPLANATION

Geologic Units

- Qa   Quaternary, surficial deposits—Alluvium and colluvium deposits
- Qls   Quaternary, surficial deposits—Landslide deposits
- Tr2   Triassic, Chinle Formation—Shinarump Member
- Tr1   Triassic, Moenkopi Formation
- P1   Permian—White Rim Sandstone, DeChelly Sandstone, Organ Rock Shale, Cedar Mesa Sandstone, Halgaito Formation, Elephant Canyon Formation

Sample site

FC-305   Site ID, refer to table 4 for site information

(Mn,Cu,Ni)   Constituents listing for those that exceed water-quality standards, see table 5. Mn indicates drinking-water standard, Cu indicates aquatic life standard

- ● Geologic background site
- ● Streambed sediment site
- ● Uranium waste dump site

Figure 5.   Location of uranium waste dump, streambed sediment, and background sites in Map 4 where solid-phase material was collected.

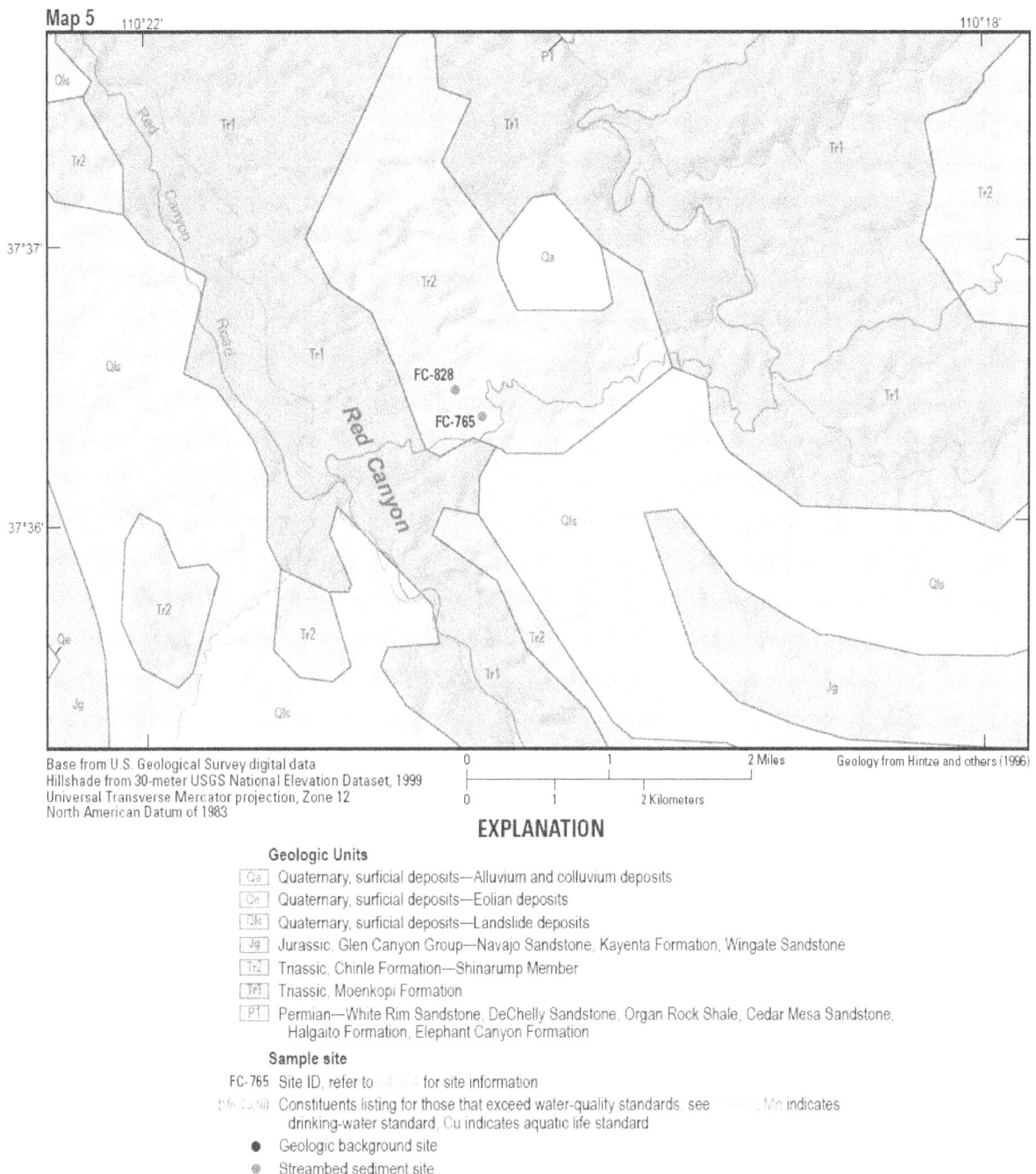

Map 5

110°22'

110°18'

37°37'

37°36'

FC-828

FC-765

Red Canyon

Base from U.S. Geological Survey digital data
Hillshade from 30-meter USGS National Elevation Dataset, 1999
Universal Transverse Mercator projection, Zone 12
North American Datum of 1983

Geology from Hintze and others (1996)

0   1   2 Miles

0   1   2 Kilometers

EXPLANATION

Geologic Units

Qa Quaternary, surficial deposits—Alluvium and colluvium deposits

Qe Quaternary, surficial deposits—Eolian deposits

Qls Quaternary, surficial deposits—Landslide deposits

Jg Jurassic, Glen Canyon Group—Navajo Sandstone, Kayenta Formation, Wingate Sandstone

Tr2 Triassic, Chinle Formation—Shinarump Member

Tr1 Triassic, Moenkopi Formation

P1 Permian—White Rim Sandstone, DeChelly Sandstone, Organ Rock Shale, Cedar Mesa Sandstone, Halgaito Formation, Elephant Canyon Formation

Sample site

FC-765 Site ID, refer to   for site information

(Mn,Cu,Ni) Constituents listing for those that exceed water-quality standards, see   . Mn indicates drinking-water standard, Cu indicates aquatic life standard

● Geologic background site

● Streambed sediment site

● Uranium waste dump site

Figure 6.   Location of uranium waste dump, streambed sediment, and background sites in Map 5 where solid-phase material was collected.

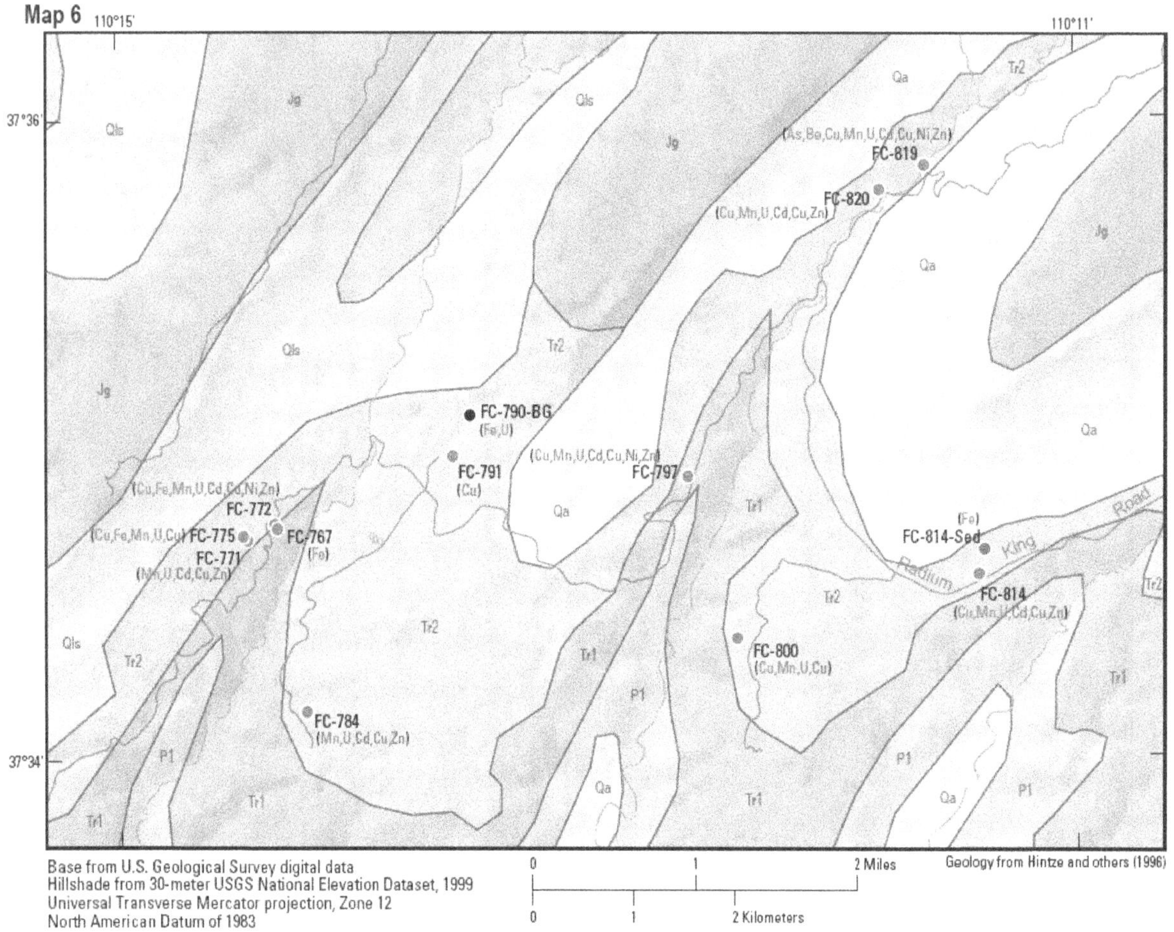

Figure 7.   Location of uranium waste dump, streambed sediment, and background sites in Map 6 where solid-phase material was collected.

Map 7

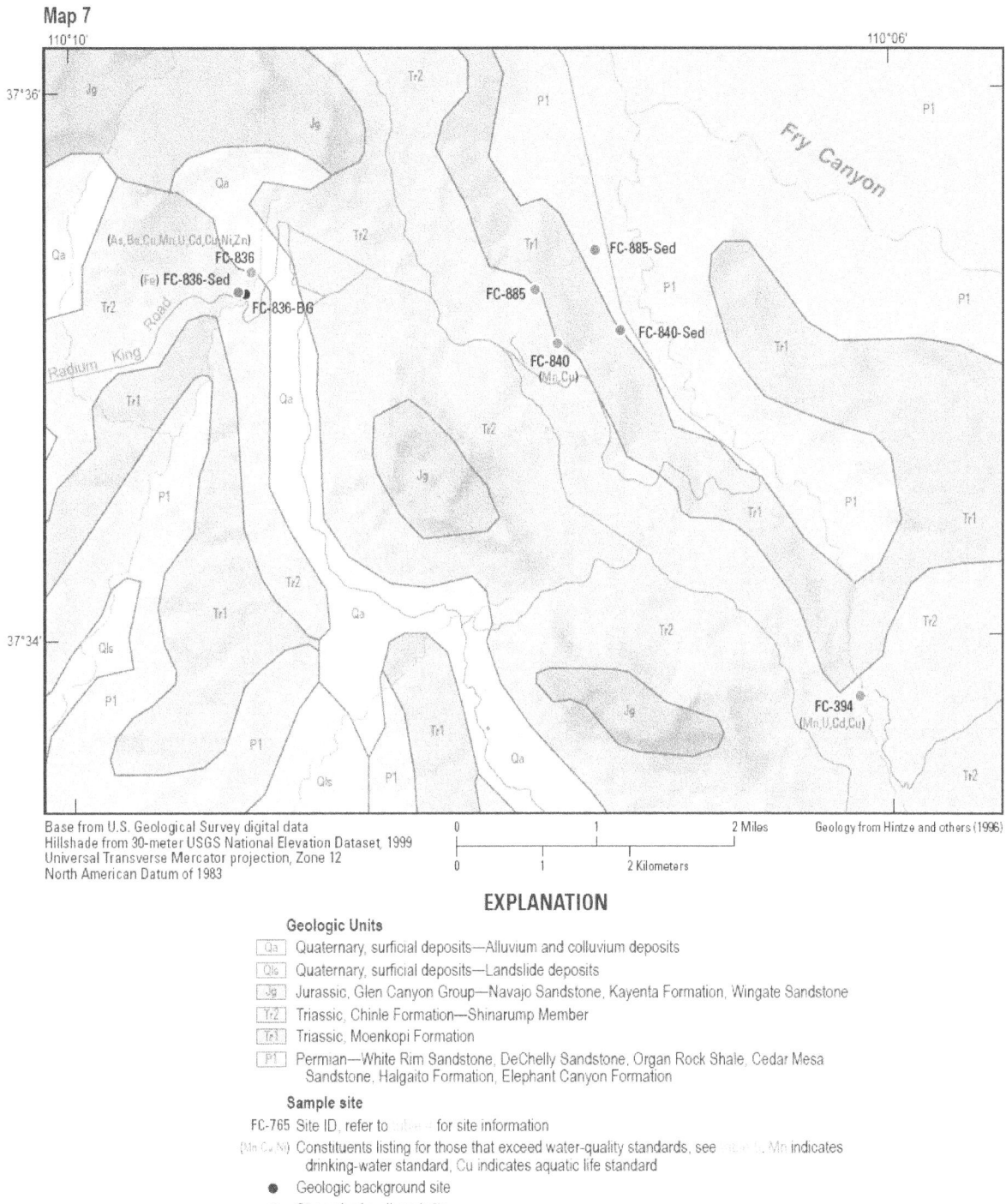

Base from U.S. Geological Survey digital data
Hillshade from 30-meter USGS National Elevation Dataset, 1999
Universal Transverse Mercator projection, Zone 12
North American Datum of 1983

Geology from Hintze and others (1996)

0   1   2 Miles

0   1   2 Kilometers

EXPLANATION

Geologic Units

Qa — Quaternary, surficial deposits—Alluvium and colluvium deposits

Qls — Quaternary, surficial deposits—Landslide deposits

Jg — Jurassic, Glen Canyon Group—Navajo Sandstone, Kayenta Formation, Wingate Sandstone

Tr2 — Triassic, Chinle Formation—Shinarump Member

Tr1 — Triassic, Moenkopi Formation

P1 — Permian—White Rim Sandstone, DeChelly Sandstone, Organ Rock Shale, Cedar Mesa Sandstone, Halgaito Formation, Elephant Canyon Formation

Sample site

FC-765 Site ID, refer to table for site information

(Mn,Cu,Ni) Constituents listing for those that exceed water-quality standards, see table 1, Mn indicates drinking-water standard, Cu indicates aquatic life standard

● Geologic background site

◉ Streambed sediment site

◉ Uranium waste dump site

Figure 8.   Location of uranium waste dump, streambed sediment, and background sites in Map 7 where solid-phase material was collected.

Map 8

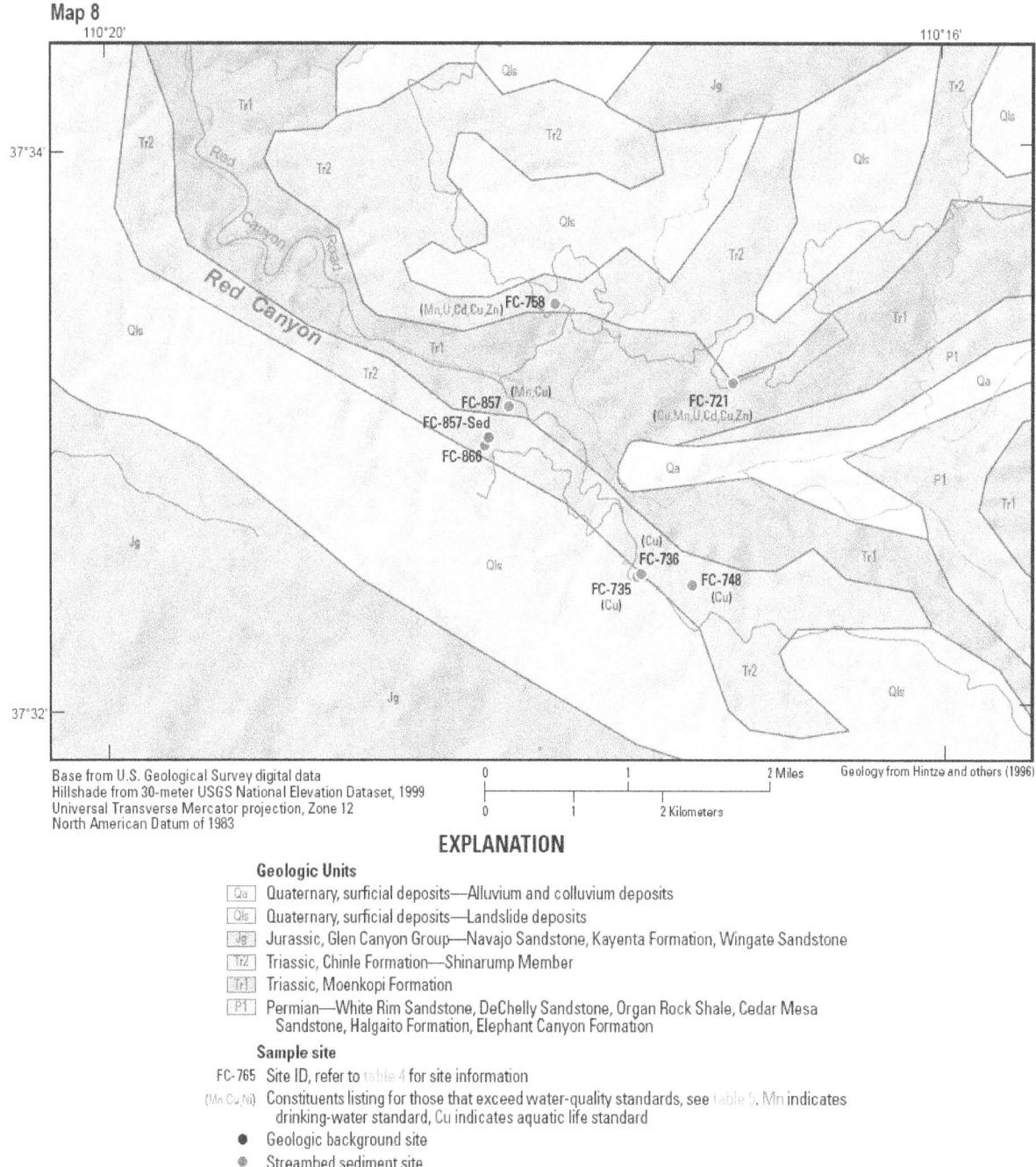

Base from U.S. Geological Survey digital data
Hillshade from 30-meter USGS National Elevation Dataset, 1999
Universal Transverse Mercator projection, Zone 12
North American Datum of 1983

Geology from Hintze and others (1996)

EXPLANATION

Geologic Units

Qa   Quaternary, surficial deposits—Alluvium and colluvium deposits

Qls   Quaternary, surficial deposits—Landslide deposits

Jg   Jurassic, Glen Canyon Group—Navajo Sandstone, Kayenta Formation, Wingate Sandstone

TrZ   Triassic, Chinle Formation—Shinarump Member

Tr1   Triassic, Moenkopi Formation

P1   Permian—White Rim Sandstone, DeChelly Sandstone, Organ Rock Shale, Cedar Mesa
       Sandstone, Halgaito Formation, Elephant Canyon Formation

Sample site

FC-765   Site ID, refer to table 4 for site information

(Mn,Cu,Ni)   Constituents listing for those that exceed water-quality standards, see table 5. Mn indicates
              drinking-water standard, Cu indicates aquatic life standard

●   Geologic background site

●   Streambed sediment site

●   Uranium waste dump site

Figure 9.   Location of uranium waste dump, streambed sediment, and background sites in Map 8 where solid-phase material was collected.

Table 2. Chemical analysis of process blank samples for selected major-ion and trace-element concentrations, Red, White, and Fry Canyons, southeastern Utah, 2007.

[Samples were analyzed at the Inductively Coupled Plasma-Mass Spectrometry Metals Analysis Laboratory at the University of Utah. Site ID, site identification; MDT, Mountain Daylight Time; fil, filtered sample; lab, laboratory analysis; mg/L, milligrams per liter; µg/L, micrograms per liter; FC, Fry Canyon area; <, less than lower reporting limit]

Site ID	Sample extraction date	Time (MDT)	Alkalinity, fil, lab (mg/L as CaCO₃)	Calcium, dissolved (mg/L)	Magnesium, dissolved (mg/L)	Potassium, dissolved (mg/L)	Sodium, dissolved (mg/L)	Sulfate, dissolved (mg/L as SO₄)	Aluminum, dissolved (µg/L)
FC-BLANK	9/17/2007	1405	<5.0	[1] 0.04	<0.004	<0.02	<0.06	<0.18	<1.0
FC-BLANK	9/19/2007	1425	<5.0	<.02	.003	<.02	<.06	<.18	<1.0
FC-BLANK	9/20/2007	1205	<5.0	.01	<.004	<.02	<.06	<.18	<1.0
FC-BLANK	9/20/2007	1305	<5.0	<.01	<.004	<.02	<.06	<.18	<1.0
FC-BLANK	9/21/2007	1130	<5.0	<.02	<.004	<.02	<.06	<.18	<1.0

Site ID	Sample extraction date	Time (MDT)	Antimony, dissolved (µg/L	Arsenic, dissolved (µg/L)	Barium, dissolved (µg/L)	Beryllium, dissolved (µg/L)	Cadmium, dissolved (µg/L)	Chromium, dissolved (µg/L)	Cobalt, dissolved (µg/L)
FC-BLANK	9/17/2007	1405	[1] 0.03	<0.05	<0.20	<0.02	[1] 0.04	<0.02	[1] 0.20
FC-BLANK	9/19/2007	1425	[1] .04	.04	<.20	<.02	<.02	[1] .06	[1] .11
FC-BLANK	9/20/2007	1205	[1] .02	<.05	<.10	<.02	.01	<.02	[1] .12
FC-BLANK	9/20/2007	1305	[1] .03	<.05	<.10	<.02	<.01	<.02	[1] .26
FC-BLANK	9/21/2007	1130	[1] .02	<.05	<.20	<.02	<.02	<.02	[1] .18

Site ID	Sample extraction date	Time (MDT)	Copper, dissolved (µg/L)	Iron, dissolved (µg/L)	Lead, dissolved (µg/L)	Manganese, dissolved (µg/L)	Molybdenum, dissolved (µg/L)	Nickel, dissolved (µg/L)	Selenium, dissolved (µg/L)
FC-BLANK	9/17/2007	1405	<0.30	<3.0	<0.07	[1] 0.43	<0.05	<0.06	<0.13
FC-BLANK	9/19/2007	1425	<.30	<3.0	<.07	[1] .25	[1] .07	<.06	<.13
FC-BLANK	9/20/2007	1205	<.30	[1] 5.0	<.07	<.20	<.05	<.06	<.13
FC-BLANK	9/20/2007	1305	<.30	<3.0	<.07	[1] .54	<.05	<.06	<.13
FC-BLANK	9/21/2007	1130	[1] .98	<3.0	<.07	[1] .35	<.05	<.06	<.13

Site ID	Sample extraction date	Time (MDT)	Silver, dissolved (µg/L)	Thallium, dissolved (µg/L)	Uranium, dissolved (µg/L)	Vanadium, dissolved (µg/L)	Zinc, dissolved (µg/L)
FC-BLANK	9/17/2007	1405	0.004	<0.01	0.04	<0.02	0.37
FC-BLANK	9/19/2007	1425	[1] .008	<.01	.04	<.02	<.60
FC-BLANK	9/20/2007	1205	<.004	<.01	<.04	<.02	<.60
FC-BLANK	9/20/2007	1305	<.004	<.01	<.04	<.02	<.60
FC-BLANK	9/21/2007	1130	<.004	<.01	.04	<.02	<.60

[1] Values exceed lower reporting limit. Sb, 0.005; Cd, 0.02; Cr, 0.02; Co, 0.04; Cu, 0.30; Fe, 3.0; Mn, 0.20; Mo, 0.05; Ag, 0.004

exception of one blank sample (5 µg/L). Concentrations of Mn ranged from 0.25 to 0.54 µg/L with a median concentration of 0.39 µg/L. All Mo concentrations were less than the lower reporting limit with the exception of one blank sample (0.07 µg/L). Concentrations of Sb ranged from 0.02 to 0.04 µg/L with a median concentration of 0.03 µg/L. Blank sample values greater than the laboratory reporting limits were still well below the water-quality standard values, which are the criteria for determining potentially hazardous sites.

Results of chemical analysis for the five replicate and associated leachate samples are presented in table 3. Although most of the results for the replicate analyses were within ±20 percent, results for a few elements in samples from selected Red, White, and Fry Canyon sites varied by more than ±20 percent: FC-343 (Ba, Cr, Fe, U); FC-394 (Al, Ca, Cr, Sb); FC-735 (Al, Fe, Pb); FC-771 (Ag, Cu, Fe, Mo, Na, Pb, U), and FC-814 (Al, Fe, Pb) (table 3). The large percentage of difference in samples may be due to variations of mineral material within a waste dump sample.

Solid-Phase Sample Digestion

Fifteen of the 45 uranium waste dump samples were analyzed by the U.S. Geological Survey Geologic Division Laboratory in Denver, Colorado, for total extractible concentration. Forty-two elements (Ag, Al, As, Ba, Be, Bi, Ca, Cd, Ce, Co, Cr, Cs, Cu, Fe, Ga, In, K, La, Li, Mg, Mn, Mo, Na, Nb, Ni, P, Pb, Rb, S, Sb, Sc, Sn, Sr, Te, Th, Ti, Tl, U, V, W, Y, and Zn) were analyzed by using inductively coupled plasma-atomic emission spectrometry (ICP-AES) following digestion of the solid sample with hydrochloric, nitric, perchloric, and hydrofluoric acids at low temperature (Crock and others, 1983). Analytical procedures and performance are presented in Briggs (2002). Selenium (Se) was analyzed by using hydride generation-atomic absorption spectrophotometry (HG-AAS) following digestion of the solid sample with nitric, hydrochloric, and sulfuric acids (Hageman and others, 2002). Mercury (Hg) was analyzed by using cold vapor-atomic absorption spectrometry (CV-AAS) following digestion of the solid sample with nitric acid and sodium dichromate (Brown and others, 2002).

Assessment of Nonpoint Source Chemical Loading Potential

Leachate Results

Trace-element concentrations in the 58 leachate samples collected from 45 uranium waste dump sites, 8 streambed sites, and 5 geologic background sites are shown in appendix A, Trace-element concentrations in the leachate samples from the uranium waste dump sites were compared with aquatic life (U.S. Environmental Protection Agency, 2007a) and drinking-

water-quality standards (U.S. Environmental Protection Agency, 2007b) (table 4). Comparisons were not made for constituents without an aquatic life or drinking-water-quality standard. The proportions of leachate samples from uranium waste dump sites that exceeded drinking-water-quality standards were As 3/45, Be 2/45, Cd 2/45, Cu 10/45, Fe 3/45, Mn 25/45, U 21/45, and Zn 1/45. The ratios of leachate samples from uranium waste dump sites that exceeded aquatic life water-quality standards were Cd 18/45, Cu 34/45, Ni 10/45, and Zn 16/45.

Drinking-water-quality standards and trace-element concentrations for leachate samples are graphically presented using boxplots in figure 10. None of the constituents had median values that exceeded both the aquatic life and drinking-water-quality standards. However, mean values for Cu, Mn, and U exceeded drinking-water-quality standards. Approximately 71 percent (32/45) of the uranium waste dump leachate samples exceeded one or more drinking-water-quality standards. Mean values for Cd, Cu, and Zn exceeded aquatic life water-quality standards. Approximately 76 percent (34/45) of uranium waste dump leachate samples exceeded aquatic life water-quality standards.

Sites where concentrations of trace elements exceeded either or both aquatic life and drinking-water-quality standards are shown using bar graphs in figures 11–19. Aquatic life and (or) drinking-water-quality standards are shown for As (fig. 11), Be (fig. 12), Cd (fig. 13), Cu (fig. 14), Fe (fig. 15), Mn (fig. 16), Ni (fig. 17), U (fig. 18), and Zn (fig. 19). Several sample sites had one or more elements that exceeded both water-quality standards. Approximately 64 percent (29/45) of the uranium waste dump samples exceeded aquatic life and drinking-water-quality standards for one or more elements analyzed. The location of sample sites, site type, constituents that exceeded one or both water-quality standards, surrounding geology, and stream hydrology are shown in detail for map areas 1 through 4 (figs. 2–5).

Two or more elements exceeded drinking-water-quality standards at sites FC-318, FC-334, FC-394, FC-687, FC-709, FC-721, FC-725, FC-727, FC-758, FC-771, FC-772, FC-775, FC-784, FC-797, FC-800, FC-814, FC-819, FC-820, and FC-836. Three elements exceeded drinking-water-quality standards at sites FC-709, FC-721, FC-797, FC-800, FC-814, and FC-820; four elements exceeded drinking-water-quality standards at sites FC-772 and FC-775; and five elements exceeded drinking-water-quality standards at sites FC-318, FC-819, and FC-836.

Two or more elements exceeded aquatic life water-quality standards at sites FC-318, FC-324, FC-334, FC-394, FC-702, FC-709, FC-710, FC-721, FC-725, FC-758, FC-771, FC-772, FC-784, FC-797, FC-814, FC-819, FC-820, and FC-836. Three elements exceeded aquatic life water-quality standards at sites FC-721, FC-758, FC-771, FC-784, FC-814, and FC-820, and four elements exceeded aquatic life water-quality standards at sites FC-318, FC-324, FC-334, FC-709, FC-710, FC-725, FC-772, FC-797, FC-819, and FC-836.

Nearly all sites with samples that exceeded drinking-water-quality standards were uranium waste dump sites. However,

Table 3. Chemical analysis of replicate and associated leachate samples from uranium waste dumps for selected major-ion and trace-element concentrations, Red, White, and Fry Canyons, southeastern Utah, 2007.

[Samples were analyzed at the Inductively Coupled Plasma-Mass Spectrometry Metals Analysis Laboratory at the University of Utah. Site ID, site identification; MDT, Mountain Daylight Time; DD.dddd, Degrees.decimal degrees; μS/cm, microsiemens per centimeter at 25 degrees Celsius; fil, filtered sample; lab, laboratory analysis; mg/L, milligrams per liter; μg/L, micrograms per liter; FC, Fry Canyon area; <, less than lower reporting limit; MI, matrix interference]

Site ID	Sample extraction date	Time (MDT)	Latitude (DD.dddd)	Longitude (DD.dddd)	Altitude (feet)	pH (standard units)	Specific Conductance (μS/cm)	Alkalinity, fil, lab (mg/L as CaCO₃)	Calcium, dissolved (mg/L)
FC-343	9/20/2007	1200	37.62942	110.10252	6,360	4.3	197	MI	24
FC-343	9/20/2007	1155	37.62942	110.10252	6,360	4.5	158	MI	22
FC-394	9/21/2007	1120	37.56295	110.1024	6,200	4.4	169	MI	[1] 17
FC-394	9/21/2007	1125	37.56295	110.1024	6,200	4.3	139	MI	[1] 14
FC-735	9/17/2007	1500	37.54135	110.29038	4,820	6.9	489	< 5.0	72
FC-735	9/17/2007	1505	37.54135	110.29038	4,820	6.8	496	5.0	76
FC-771	9/19/2007	1420	37.5788	110.23853	5,280	5.6	453	< 5.0	59
FC-771	9/19/2007	1415	37.5788	110.23853	5,280	5.6	468	< 5.0	65
FC-814	9/20/2007	1255	37.57625	110.18958	5,720	5.8	204	< 5.0	18
FC-814	9/20/2007	1300	37.57625	110.18958	5,720	5.6	217	< 5.0	19

Site ID	Sample extraction date	Magnesium, dissolved (mg/L)	Potassium, dissolved (mg/L)	Sodium, dissolved (mg/L)	Sulfate, dissolved (mg/L as SO₄)	Aluminum, dissolved (μg/L)	Antimony, dissolved (μg/L)	Arsenic, dissolved (μg/L)	Barium, dissolved (μg/L)
FC-343	9/20/2007	1.23	2.2	0.11	67	208	0.02	0.2	[1] 16
FC-343	9/20/2007	1.16	2.2	.10	74	170	.02	.2	[1] 12
FC-394	9/21/2007	1.14	2.2	.5	57	[1] 93	[1] .09	1.7	10
FC-394	9/21/2007	0.95	2.1	.43	48	[1] 70	[1] .06	1.8	9.4
FC-735	9/17/2007	0.53	2.5	.40	182	[1] 8.3	.09	1.3	24
FC-735	9/17/2007	0.55	2.6	.40	191	[1] 5.8	.09	1.4	26
FC-771	9/19/2007	5.05	2.3	[1] .67	171	31	.10	1.6	9.9
FC-771	9/19/2007	4.75	2.1	[1] .51	190	34	.11	1.8	8.5
FC-814	9/20/2007	2.34	1.3	3.1	65	[1] 18	.16	.4	7.8
FC-814	9/20/2007	2.48	1.4	2.8	69	[1] 35	.17	.5	8.6

Site ID	Sample extraction date	Cadmium, dissolved (μg/L)	Chromium, dissolved (μg/L)	Cobalt, dissolved (μg/L)	Copper, dissolved (μg/L)	Iron, dissolved (μg/L)	Lead, dissolved (μg/L)	Manganese, dissolved (μg/L)	Molybdenum, dissolved (μg/L)
FC-343	9/20/2007	0.09	[1] 0.04	15	6.1	[1] 9.0	[1] 0.02	164	<0.05
FC-343	9/20/2007	.08	[1] .13	13	5.3	[1] 5.0	[1] <.07	155	<.05
FC-394	9/21/2007	.26	[1] .02	23	1,000	6.0	.03	74	.65
FC-394	9/21/2007	.23	[1] .03	19	840	6.0	.03	64	.60
FC-735	9/17/2007	<.02	.10	0.88	22	[1] 24	[1] .06	7.0	.18
FC-735	9/17/2007	<.02	.10	0.84	21	[1] 19	[1] .04	7.0	.17
FC-771	9/19/2007	.54	.08	85	[1] 960	[1] 15	[1] .12	144	[1] .13
FC-771	9/19/2007	.49	.09	74	[1] 700	[1] 42	[1] .09	130	[1] .16
FC-814	9/20/2007	.49	.05	23	3,100	[1] 4.0	[1] <.07	122	.81
FC-814	9/20/2007	.52	.05	25	3,300	[1] 16	[1] .13	127	.71

Table 3. Chemical analysis of replicate and associated leachate samples from uranium waste dumps for selected major-ion and trace-element concentrations, Red, White, and Fry Canyons, southeastern Utah, 2007.—Continued

[Samples were analyzed at the Inductively Coupled Plasma-Mass Spectrometry Metals Analysis Laboratory at the University of Utah. Site ID, site identification; MDT, Mountain Daylight Time; DD.dddd, Degrees.decimal degrees; µS/cm, microsiemens per centimeter at 25 degrees Celsius; fil, filtered sample; lab, laboratory analysis; mg/L, milligrams per liter; µg/L, micrograms per liter; FC, Fry Canyon area; <, less than lower reporting limit; MI, matrix interference]

Site ID	Sample extraction date	Nickel, dissolved (µg/L)	Selenium, dissolved (µg/L)	Silver, dissolved (µg/L)	Thallium, dissolved (µg/L)	Uranium, dissolved (µg/L)	Vanadium, dissolved (µg/L)	Zinc, dissolved (µg/L)
FC-343	9/20/2007	14	<0.13	<0.004	0.11	[1] 3.8	0.04	30
FC-343	9/20/2007	12	<.13	<.004	.11	[1] 2.9	.04	26
FC-394	9/21/2007	16	.18	.02	.17	46	.07	71
FC-394	9/21/2007	14	.15	.02	.17	40	.07	60
FC-735	9/17/2007	0.70	.11	<.004	.05	1.7	.36	1.1
FC-735	9/17/2007	0.71	.12	<.004	.05	1.8	.33	0.98
FC-771	9/19/2007	46	.33	[1] .03	.07	[1] 175	.21	275
FC-771	9/19/2007	40	.32	[1] .01	.07	[1] 138	.24	241
FC-814	9/20/2007	14	<.13	.02	.06	140	.11	145
FC-814	9/20/2007	15	<.13	.02	.06	139	.12	153

[1] Replicate samples exceeding ± 20 percent

Table 4. U.S. Environmental Protection Agency drinking-water-quality standards and aquatic life water-quality standards.

[µg/L, micrograms per liter; NA, not applicable]

Element	[1]Drinking-water standard concentration (µg/L)	[2]Aquatic life water standard concentration (µg/L)
Antimony (Sb)	6.0	NA
Arsenic (As)	10	150
Barium (Ba)	2,000	NA
Beryllium (Be)	4.0	NA
Cadmium (Cd)	5.0	[3]0.25
Chromium (Cr)	100	NA
Copper (Cu)	1,300	[3]9.0
Iron (Fe)	300	NA
Lead (Pb)	15	[3]2.5
Manganese (Mn)	50	NA
Mercury (Hg)	2.0	0.77
Molybdenum (Mo)	NA	NA
Nickel (Ni)	NA	[3]52
Selenium (Se)	50	5.0
Silver (Ag)	100	NA
Thallium (Tl)	2.0	NA
Uranium (U)	30	NA
Vanadium (V)	NA	NA
Zinc (Zn)	5,000	[3]120

[1]Drinking-water-quality standards (U.S. Environmental Protection Agency, 2007b)

[2]Aquatic life water-quality standards (U.S. Environmental Protection Agency, 2007a)

[3]Aquatic life standard is based on a hardness value of 100 µg/L

two background samples and three streambed-sediment samples also exceeded water-quality standards. Iron and uranium concentrations exceeded the drinking-water-quality standard in the background sample from site FC-790-BG and arsenic concentrations exceeded the drinking-water-quality standard and copper concentrations exceeded the aquatic life water-quality standard in the background sample from site FC-682-BG. Iron concentrations exceeded drinking-water-quality standards at streambed-sediment sites FC-334-SED, FC-814-SED, and FC-836-SED, and manganese concentrations exceeded the drinking water-quality standard from site FC-710-SED. Standards were not exceeded in samples from other background or streambed sites. Most uranium waste dump sites are located in or near ephemeral streams that would likely minimize their contaminant contribution to perennial streams. Select trace element concentrations for all samples exceeded water-quality standards for both drinking water and aquatic life at sites FC-305, FC-318, FC-709, FC-721, FC-772, FC-775, FC-797, FC-814, FC-819, FC-820, and FC-836, located in Red Canyon. Dissolved copper concentrations were largest in samples from sites FC-721, FC-772, FC-797, FC-814, FC-819, FC-820, and FC-836, ranging from 3,300 µg/L (FC-814) to 92,000 µg/L (FC-772) (fig. 14). Dissolved uranium concentrations were largest in samples from sites FC-772 and FC-819, ranging from 990 µg/L (FC-819) to 1,200 µg/L (FC-772) (fig. 18).

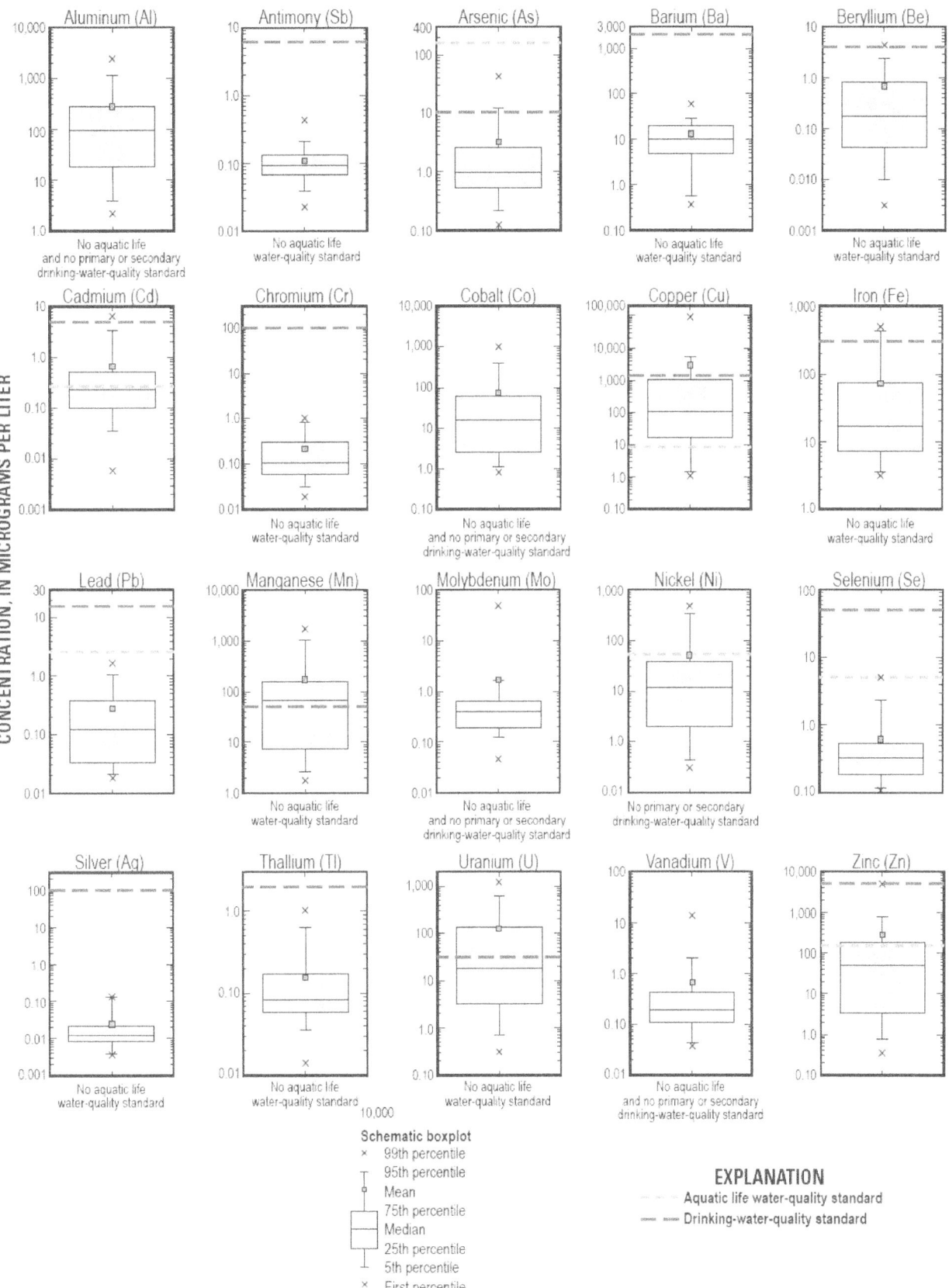

Figure 10. Concentrations of dissolved trace elements in leachate extractions from the 45 uranium waste dump samples collected from Red, White, and Fry Canyons, southeastern Utah, 2007.

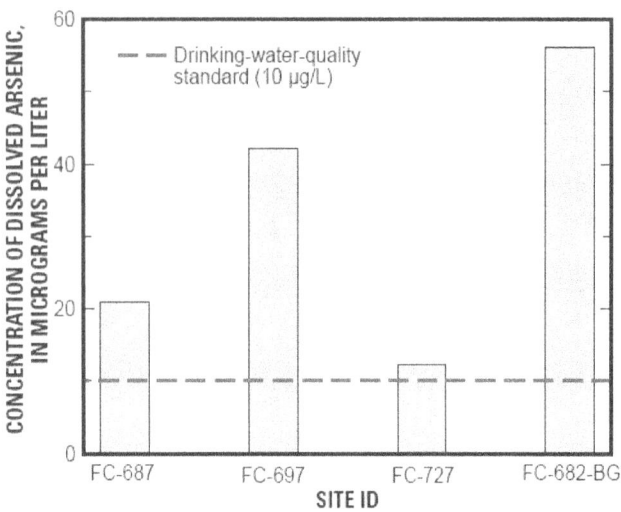

Figure 11.   Concentrations of dissolved arsenic in uranium waste dump leachate samples that exceeded aquatic life and drinking-water-quality standards, Red, White, and Fry Canyons, southeastern Utah, 2007.

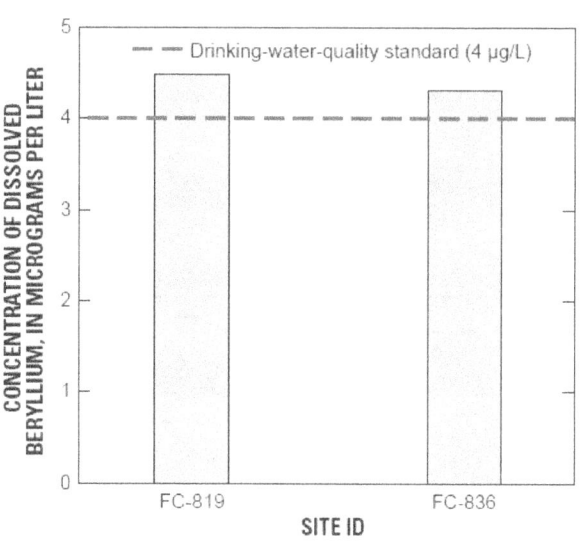

Figure 12.   Concentrations of dissolved beryllium in uranium waste dump leachate samples that exceeded drinking-water-quality standards, Red, White, and Fry Canyons, southeastern Utah, 2007.

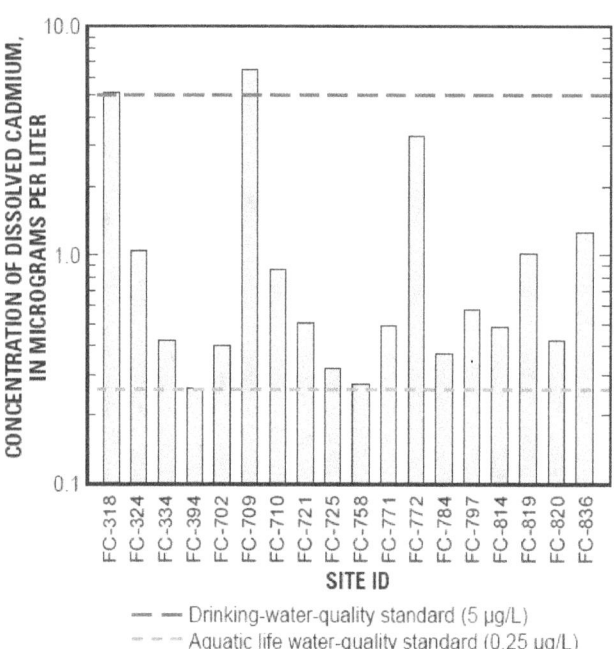

Figure 13.   Concentrations of dissolved cadmium in uranium waste dump leachate samples that exceeded aquatic life and drinking-water-quality standards, Red, White, and Fry Canyons, southeastern Utah, 2007.

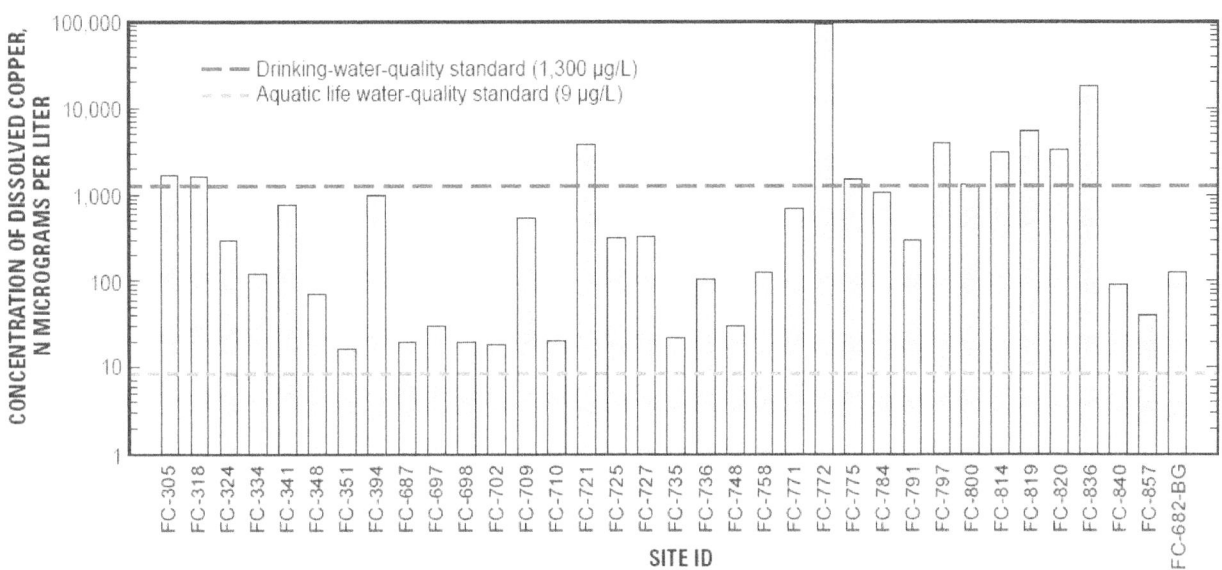

Figure 14. Concentrations of dissolved copper in uranium waste dump leachate samples that exceeded aquatic life and drinking-water-quality standards, Red, White, and Fry Canyons, southeastern Utah, 2007.

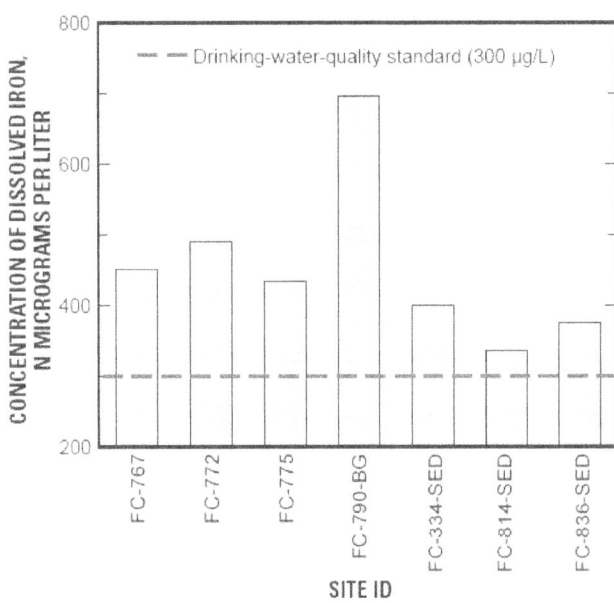

Figure 15. Concentrations of dissolved iron in uranium waste dump leachate samples that exceeded drinking-water-quality standards, Red, White, and Fry Canyons, southeastern Utah, 2007.

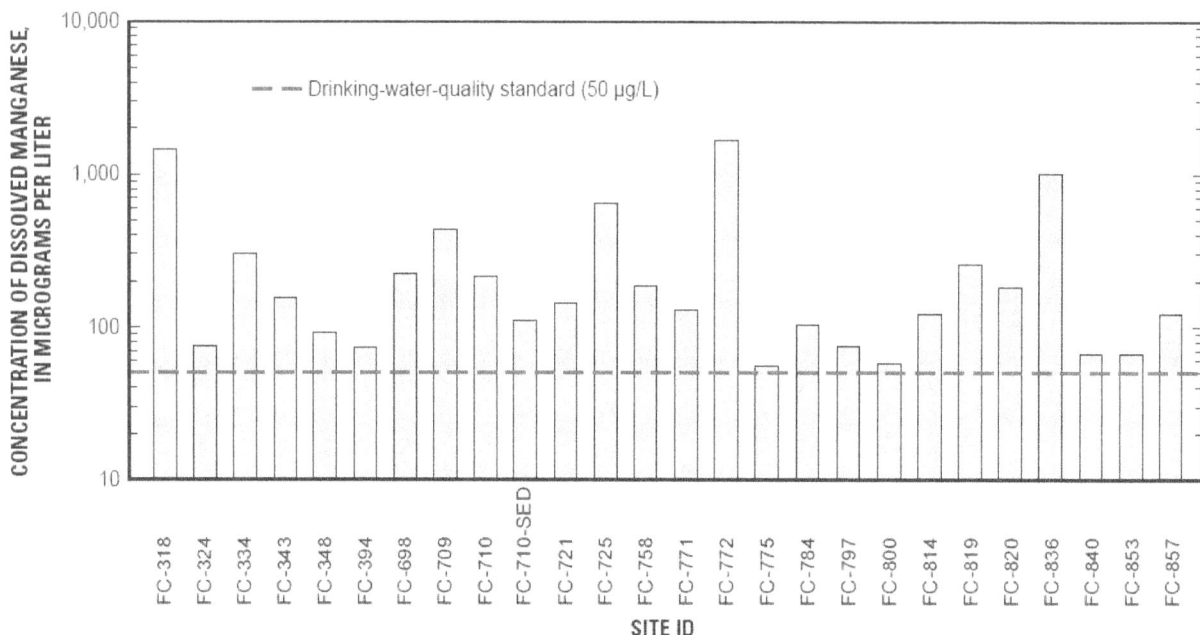

Figure 16. Concentrations of dissolved manganese in uranium waste dump leachate samples that exceeded drinking-water-quality standards, Red, White, and Fry Canyons, southeastern Utah, 2007.

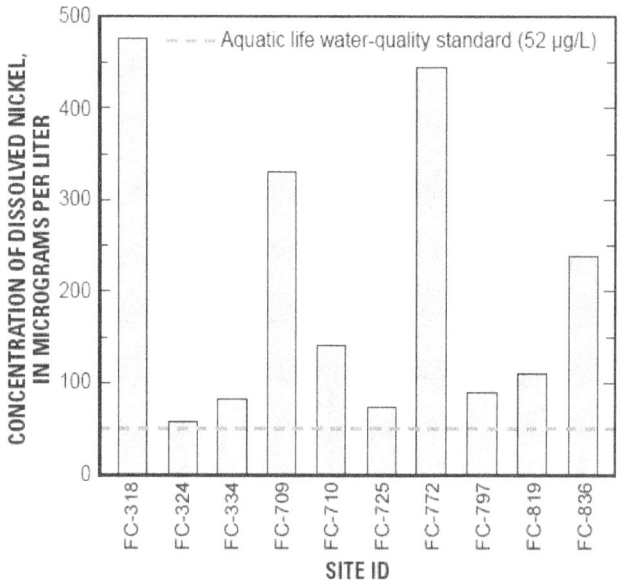

Figure 17. Concentrations of dissolved nickel in uranium waste dump leachate samples that exceeded aquatic life water-quality standards, Red, White, and Fry Canyons, southeastern Utah, 2007.

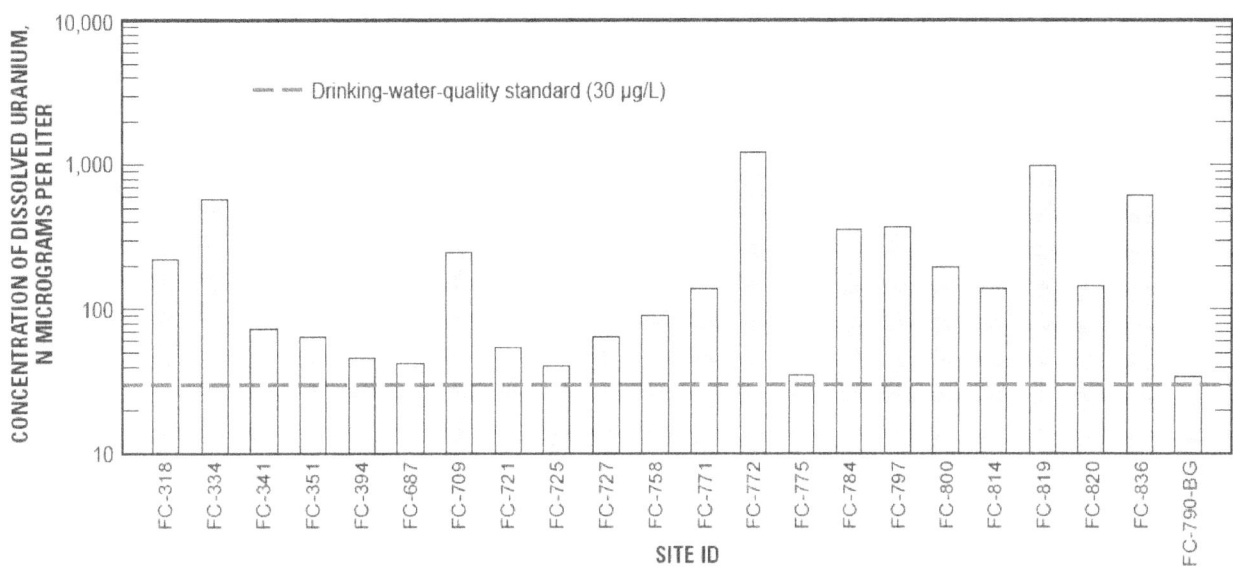

Figure 18. Concentrations of dissolved uranium in uranium waste dump leachate samples that exceeded drinking-water-quality standards, Red, White, and Fry Canyons, southeastern Utah, 2007.

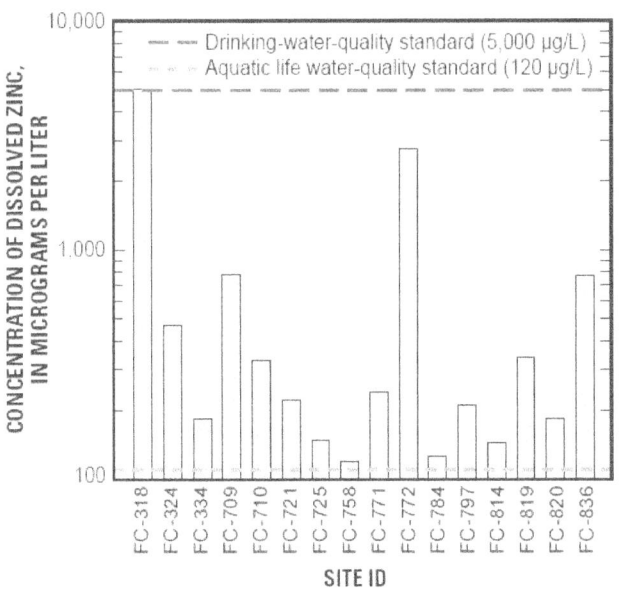

Figure 19. Concentrations of dissolved zinc in uranium waste dump leachate samples that exceeded drinking-water-quality standards, Red, White, and Fry Canyons, southeastern Utah, 2007.

StreamStats Analysis of Waste Dump Sites

Periodic rainfall events may fill ephemeral stream drainages with water and transport some of the waste dump material off site. Because of the episodic nature of streamflow in the Red, White, and Fry Canyons, no permanent gaging stations are currently recording flow. A set of multiple-linear regression equations have been developed for the State of Utah to estimate peak flows in ungaged drainages. All uranium waste dump sites in Red, White, and Fry Canyons are located within EPA Region 6, and regression equations for 2-, 100-, and 500-year recurrence interval peak flows are given below (Kenney and others, 2007):

$$PK2 = 4.150 DRNAREA^{0.553} (ELEV/1,000)^{-2.45} \qquad (1)$$

$$PK100 = 115,000 DRNAREA^{0.391} (ELEV/1,000)^{-2.58} \qquad (2)$$

$$PK500 = 258,000 DRNAREA^{0.344} (ELEV/1,000)^{-2.65} \qquad (3)$$

where,

PK	is the peak flow; number following PK represents recurrence interval, in years,
DRNAREA	is the drainage area, in square miles, and
ELEV	is the mean basin elevation, in feet.

The parameters and equations for drainage areas throughout Utah were made into an interactive website, StreamStats (Ries and others, 2004). All sample sites were input into the USGS Utah StreamStats website at *http://streamstatsags.cr.usgs.gov/ut_ss/default.aspx?stabbr=ut&dt=1241905018973* to determine the drainage basin characteristics contributing to runoff at the uranium waste dump sites (table 5). Four uranium waste dump sites with the largest drainage basin areas on the basis of the StreamStats delineation were FC-394 (2.8 mi²),

Table 5. Drainage area characteristics associated with uranium waste dump samples, Red, White, Blue Notch, and Fry Canyons, southeastern Utah.

[Site ID, site identification; DD.dddd, Degrees.decimal degrees; PK 2, 2-year peak flow; PK 100, 100-year peak flow; PK 500, 500-year peak flow; FC, Fry Canyon area; BG, background; SED, sediment; NA, not applicable]

Site ID	Latitude (DD.dddd)	Longitude (DD.dddd)	Altitude (feet)	Mean Annual Precip- itation (inches)	Average Basin Slope (percent)	Area (square miles)	Mean Basin Elevation (feet)	Area Covered by Herbaceous Upland (percent)	Drainage Canyon	PK 2 (cubic feet per second)	PK 100 (cubic feet per second)	PK 500 (cubic feet per second)
FC-305	37.6302	110.16847	5,820	12	19	0.0002	5,820	0	Fry	NA	NA	NA
FC-305-BG	37.62957	110.16848	5,820	12	20	.001	5,850	0	Fry	NA	NA	NA
FC-314	37.65202	110.1831	5,860	9.4	46	.06	6,130	1.1	White	10	351	794
FC-318	37.66235	110.1984	5,660	10	44	.04	6,070	0	White	8.5	314	722
FC-324	37.63702	110.11743	6,140	11	28	.0006	6,250	0	Fry	0.76	56	155
FC-334	37.6311	110.11207	6,220	11	10	.04	6,350	0	Fry	7 2	267	615
FC-334-SED	37.63092	110.11258	6,220	11	10	.04	6,350	0	Fry	7 5	276	633
FC-341	37.63183	110.1079	6,280	11	17	.006	6,290	0	White	2.6	132	332
FC-343	37.62942	110.10252	6,360	11	17	.0008	6,340	0	White	0.88	61	167
FC-348	37.63253	110.10883	6,280	11	24	.0003	6,260	0	White	0.57	45	129
FC-351	37.63408	110.11718	6,180	11	28	.001	6,230	0	Fry	1 2	76	205
FC-355	37.6337	110.1177	6,100	11	56	.001	6,180	0	Fry	1 3	82	219
FC-394	37.56295	110.1024	6,200	13	14	2.8	6,690	0.64	Fry	69	1,270	2,380
FC-678	37.75673	110.2982	5,120	8.8	57	.04	5,430	2.3	White	11	414	961
FC-682-BG	37.76337	110.35008	4,480	NA	NA	NA	NA	NA	Blue Notch	NA	NA	NA
FC-687	37.67682	110.13437	6,240	11	33	.004	6,300	0	White	NA	NA	NA
FC-697	37.67545	110.22558	5,280	10	36	.07	5,740	0	White	13	437	985
FC-698	37.72662	110.20078	5,720	8.9	34	.006	5,840	0	White	NA	NA	NA
FC-702	37.70107	110.31898	4,600	9.6	28	3.1	5,510	12	Red	119	2,190	4,140
FC-709	37.70945	110.3116	4,740	9.8	28	.007	4,970	0	Red	5.4	269	679
FC-709-BG	37.7099	110.31173	4,740	9.5	28	2.0	5,680	9.3	Red	86	1,710	3,280
FC-709-SED	37.70978	110.31273	4,740	9.5	28	2.0	5,680	9.3	Red	87	1,710	3,290
FC-710	37.73473	110.34942	4,520	8.0	42	.04	4,840	1.5	Blue Notch	15	558	1,300
FC-710-SED	37.73517	110.34957	4,520	8.0	42	.04	4,830	1.5	Blue Notch	15	567	1,320
FC-716	37.69552	110.32375	4,600	9.8	32	.07	5,080	2.2	Red	17	604	1,370
FC-721	37.55278	110.28272	4,880	8.3	16	.04	4,990	26	Red	14	519	1,210
FC-725	37.72652	110.19988	5,760	8.9	38	.03	6,040	37	White	7 2	279	652
FC-727	37.72618	110.19722	5,800	8.9	25	.002	5,830	0	White	1.7	102	273
FC-735	37 54135	110.29038	4,820	8.9	23	.06	5,010	11	Red	17	609	1,390
FC-736	37 54418	110.29027	4,820	NA	NA	NA	NA	NA	Red	NA	NA	NA
FC-748	37 54079	110.28602	4,840	10	36	.33	5,340	7.5	Red	38	1,000	2,100
FC-758	37 55754	110.29674	4,800	8.8	30	.26	5,330	27	Red	33	910	1,940
FC-765	37.60642	110.33933	4,400	6.9	26	.001	4,510	0	Red	2.8	184	505
FC-767	37 57825	110.24085	5,360	10	38	.04	5,630	27	Red	10	374	866
FC-771	37 5788	110.23853	5,280	10	40	.14	5,810	22	Red	18	548	1,200
FC-772	37.57905	110.2387	5,280	10	41	.13	5,830	22	Red	18	548	1,200
FC-775	37.57822	110.24068	5,360	10	39	.04	5,610	33	Red	10	374	866
FC-784	37.5693	110.23653	5,280	9.6	6.7	.10	5,470	2.4	Red	18	583	1,290
FC-790-BG	37 58467	110.22487	5,440	10	27	.03	5,750	4.6	Red	8.9	340	789
FC-791	37 58252	110.22608	5,400	10	16	.007	5,590	0	Red	4.1	199	499
FC-797	37 5814	110.20973	5,460	10	17	.02	5,570	24	Red	7.8	317	752
FC-800	37 57296	110.20635	5,440	9.9	15	.04	5,560	0	Red	11	402	927
FC-814	37.57625	110.18958	5,720	10	9 1	.001	5,640	0	Red	1 5	99	269
FC-814-SED	37.57753	110.18917	5,720	10	27	.05	5,880	21	Red	11	379	861
FC-819	37.5975	110.19318	5,680	11	23	2.9	6,590	6.3	Red	74	1,340	2,510
FC-820	37.59627	110.19628	5,640	11	24	3.1	6,560	6.2	Red	77	1,390	2,600
FC-828	37.60802	110.34152	4,360	6.9	16	.0001	4,460	0	Red	NA	NA	NA
FC-836	37.58912	110.15163	5,920	11	24	.53	6,320	14	Red	32	777	1,580
FC-836-BG	37.58785	110.15215	5,920	11	24	.53	6,320	14	Red	32	777	1,580

Table 5. Drainage area characteristics associated with uranium waste dump samples, Red, White, Blue Notch, and Fry Canyons, southeastern Utah.—Continued

[Site ID, site identification; DD.dddd, Degrees.decimal degrees; PK 2, 2-year peak flow; PK 100, 100-year peak flow; PK 500, 500-year peak flow; FC, Fry Canyon area; BG, background; SED, sediment; NA, not applicable]

Site ID	Latitude (DD.dddd)	Longitude (DD.dddd)	Altitude (feet)	Mean Annual Precipitation (inches)	Average Basin Slope (percent)	Area (square miles)	Mean Basin Elevation (feet)	Area Covered by Herbaceous Upland (percent)	Drainage Canyon	PK 2 (cubic feet per second)	PK 100 (cubic feet per second)	PK 500 (cubic feet per second)
FC-836-SED	37.58788	110 15255	5,920	11	24	0.53	6,320	14	Red	32	777	1,580
FC-840	37.5846	110 12691	6,000	11	31	.14	6,330	1.1	Fry	15	456	987
FC-840-SED	37.58537	110 12185	6,000	11	30	.21	6,190	1.9	Fry	20	566	1,200
FC-853	37.76457	110 36922	4,280	8.1	37	.49	4,890	15	Blue Notch	57	1,450	3,010
FC-857	37.54968	110 30207	4,800	8.8	34	.21	5,190	7.0	Red	31	892	1,920
FC-857-SED	37.5515	110 30043	4,800	8.8	32	.27	5,070	6.3	Red	38	1,050	2,230
FC-866	37.5492	110 30237	4,760	8.8	34	.21	5,190	6.6	Red	31	892	1,920
FC-885	37.5879	110 12867	5,980	11	19	.0002	5,940	0	Fry	0.52	44	129
FC-885-SED	37.59027	110 12382	5,980	11	24	.04	5,750	0	Fry	10	374	859

FC-702 (3.1 mi^2), FC-819 (2.9 mi^2), and FC-820 (3.1 mi^2). Six uranium waste dump sites with steep average basin slopes (more than 40 percent) were FC-314, FC-318, FC-355, FC-678, FC-710, and FC-772. Average basin slopes for these sites were 46, 44, 56, 57, 42, and 41 percent, respectively.

The valid range for the regression equations (1–3) is a drainage area between 0.87 and 532 mi^2 and a mean basin elevation between 4,300 and 9,380 ft. Many drainage area values were less than the minimum value of 0.87 mi^2, but all mean basin elevation values fell within the valid range (table 5). Peak flows estimated from values outside of valid regression equation ranges are extrapolations with unknown errors. The errors given for values within the valid range for PK2, PK100, and PK500 are 110, 61, and 66 percent average standard error of prediction and 1.44, 13, and 15 equivalent years of record, respectively (Kenney and others, 2007).

Human Health Hazard Assessment

Fifteen uranium waste dump samples were analyzed for total digestible metal concentration (table 6). Samples were analyzed for major (Ca, K, Mg, Na, P, S), trace (Ag, Al, As, Ba, Be, Bi, Cd, Co, Cr, Cs, Cu, Fe, Ga, Hg, In, Li, Mn, Mo, Nb, Ni, Pb, Rb, Sb, Sc, Se, Sn, Sr, Te, Th, Ti, Tl, U, V, W, Y, Zn), and rare earth elements (Ce, La).

A relation between leachate and total digestible uranium concentration has been determined based on a regression equation with all known data (fig. 20):

$$U_{total\ (ppm)} = 28.434\ \ln (U_{leachate\ (\mu g/L)}) + 59.093 \qquad (4)$$

Equation 4 was used to determine the total concentration for the uranium waste dump sites with only a leachate analysis (table 7). Data from waste dump site FC-721 was not used to compute the regression equation because it was determined to be an outlier.

Three soil screening levels (SSL) for various exposure durations were determined for the combined carcinogenic effects of uranium and radium as radionuclides based on calculations made with RESRAD 6.5, a computer model designed to estimate radiation doses and risks from residual radioactive materials (Yu and others, 1993). Soil screening levels were determined with respect to a probable concentration of radium and all other uranium decay series radionuclides set to secular equilibrium with radium-226. In the Colorado Plateau region uranium deposits, secular equilibrium between radium and uranium is typically not observed, and in many places, uranium deposits are depleted in radium with respect to uranium by daughter products leached from primary uranium minerals by forming secondary minerals from changing groundwater conditions and oxidation (Stern and Stieff, 1959). Since the sites in this study were not sampled for radium, a concentration range for radium was considered. The equilibrium radium concentration, or high end concentration, assumes that radium is in secular equilibrium with uranium in any waste dump pile. The leached concentration, or low end concentration, assumes that radium activities are approximately 57 percent of uranium activities in any waste dump pile. The radium-uranium ratio of 0.57 is derived from a similar study conducted in Brown's Hole, Utah, where sites were sampled for radium and uranium (Tom Marston, U.S. Geological Survey, written commun. 2010).

Soil screening levels were evaluated for a maximum annual radiation dosage of 15 mrem per year (U.S. Environmental Protection Agency, 1997a). Several exposure pathways were considered in the model: direct external exposure to contaminated soils, internal exposure to inhaled dust, and internal exposure by ingestion of contaminated soils. RESRAD also considers exposures from ingested plants grown in contaminated soils, from ingested meat derived from livestock fed with contaminated feed or water, from drinking water directly, and from ingested fish from a contaminated body of water. These pathways were not included based on

Table 6. Chemical analysis of total extractible from samples from uranium waste dumps for selected major-ion and trace-element concentrations, Red, White, and Fry Canyons, southeastern Utah, 2007.

[Samples were analyzed at the U.S. Geological Survey Geologic Discipline Laboratory, Denver, Colorado. Site ID, site identification; MDT, Mountain Daylight Time; DD.dddd, Degrees.decimal degrees; %, percent; ppm, parts per million; FC, Fry Canyon area; <, less than lower reporting limit]

Site ID	Sample extraction date	Time (MDT)	Latitude (DD.dddd)	Longitude (DD.dddd)	Altitude (feet)	Aluminum, total (%)	Antimony, total (ppm)	Arsenic, total (ppm)	Barium, total (ppm)	Beryllium, total (ppm)	Bismuth, total (ppm)	Cadmium, total (ppm)
FC-318	9/21/2007	1045	37.66235	110.1984	5,660	4 5	1.3	74	240	2.3	0.17	0.50
FC-324	9/21/2007	1140	37.63702	110.11743	6,140	3 1	1.5	72	430	1.7	.09	.50
FC-334	9/20/2007	1240	37.6311	110.11207	6,220	3.6	1.7	110	240	1.1	.15	< .10
FC-343	9/20/2007	1155	37.62942	110.10252	6,360	6.4	0.63	45	240	2.2	.23	< .10
FC-355	9/20/2007	1225	37.6337	110.1177	6,100	3.6	1.6	120	480	1.5	< .04	.30
FC-697	9/17/2007	1445	37.67545	110.22558	5,280	2 2	1.4	200	180	1.2	.07	< .10
FC-721	9/19/2007	1435	37.55278	110.28272	4,880	6.7	1.7	97	730	3.4	.09	.20
FC-765	9/21/2007	1105	37.60642	110.33933	4,400	2.6	0.44	25	320	0.80	.11	.10
FC-771	9/19/2007	1415	37.5788	110.23853	5,280	5 9	1.0	100	360	3.5	.19	.20
FC-772	9/20/2007	1245	37.57905	110.2387	5,280	3 3	0.97	71	380	1.5	.14	.30
FC-775	9/20/2007	1145	37.57822	110.24068	5,360	5 9	1.4	78	320	3.2	.20	.10
FC-797	9/21/2007	1155	37.5814	110.20973	5,460	4 9	0.80	57	330	1.9	.20	< .10
FC-819	9/19/2007	1450	37.5975	110.19318	5,680	5 5	1.7	100	420	3.0	.19	.10
FC-836	9/21/2007	1110	37.58912	110.15163	5,920	5 1	1.4	100	510	2.1	< .04	< .10
FC-853	9/21/2007	1040	37.76457	110.36922	4,280	2.4	1.1	230	550	1.1	.38	.30

Site ID	Calcium, total (%)	Cerium, total (ppm)	Cesium, total (ppm)	Chromium, total (ppm)	Cobalt, total (ppm)	Copper, total (ppm)	Gallium, total (ppm)	Indium, total (ppm)	Iron, total (%)	Lanthanum, total (ppm)	Lithium, total (ppm)	Lead, total (ppm)	Magnesium, total (%)
FC-318	0.62	45	6.0	48	100	660	10	0.04	1.9	22	27	30	0.31
FC-324	1.0	28	< 5.0	34	74	2,600	7.3	.02	1.2	14	20	35	.23
FC-334	.44	50	< 5.0	39	4.4	37	8.2	.03	2.2	27	26	41	.12
FC-343	.17	66	< 5.0	44	21	23	16	.05	2.2	34	44	28	.16
FC-355	.98	36	< 5.0	32	22	62	8.3	.03	1.3	17	25	100	.36
FC-697	.23	28	< 5.0	27	52	3,600	4.5	< .02	1.0	12	14	22	.16
FC-721	.99	100	6.0	49	45	2,600	15	.06	3.3	51	42	47	.97
FC-765	1.0	35	< 5.0	32	47	260	5.5	.02	1.2	18	17	11	.38
FC-771	.99	53	5.0	57	97	1,700	14	.05	3.0	27	45	24	.86
FC-772	.56	34	< 5.0	32	64	8,900	8.2	.03	2.1	16	32	29	.43
FC-775	.69	54	< 5.0	55	48	1,500	13	.04	2.2	28	44	30	.52
FC-797	.04	140	< 5.0	56	7.3	350	11	.05	1.4	65	34	24	.14
FC-819	.23	68	< 5.0	56	18	630	15	.05	3.0	34	32	40	.52
FC-836	.18	72	< 5.0	31	11	1,000	11	.03	2.0	33	30	29	.34
FC-853	1.9	50	< 5.0	22	270	180	7.7	.02	2.8	22	16	44	.13

Table 6. Chemical analysis of total extractible from samples from uranium waste dumps for selected major-ion and trace-element concentrations, Red, White, and Fry Canyons, southeastern Utah, 2007.—Continued

[Samples were analyzed at the U.S. Geological Survey Geologic Discipline Laboratory, Denver, Colorado. Site ID, site identification; MDT, Mountain Daylight Time; DD.dddd, Degrees.decimal degrees; %, percent; ppm, parts per million; FC, Fry Canyon area; <, less than lower reporting limit]

Site ID	Manganese, total (ppm)	Mercury, total (ppm)	Molybdenum, total (ppm)	Nickel, total (ppm)	Niobium, total (ppm)	Phosphorus, total (ppm)	Potassium, total (%)	Rubidium, total (ppm)	Scandium, total (ppm)	Selenium, total (ppm)	Silver, total (ppm)	Sodium, total (%)
FC-318	210	0.01	12	61	7.4	420	1.2	56	9.7	0.50	< 1.0	0.08
FC-324	120	.03	21	50	4.2	230	1.0	39	5.2	< .20	< 1.0	.07
FC-334	26	.01	30	5.5	5.1	290	0.69	30	6.4	.30	< 1.0	.07
FC-343	110	.02	13	16	11	370	1.2	71	11	.50	< 1.0	11
FC-355	200	.01	21	17	5.2	280	1.1	40	5.5	.90	< 1.0	.04
FC-697	160	.01	2.5	18	2.8	120	0.76	24	3.9	.20	2.0	11
FC-721	270	.08	16	33	8.5	690	2.6	110	12	.40	< 1.0	.60
FC-765	220	< .01	1.2	23	3.3	190	0.62	27	4.5	.20	< 1.0	.05
FC-771	340	.02	3.9	46	8.1	490	1.7	77	13	.30	< 1.0	36
FC-772	130	.01	16	27	4.8	250	0.91	33	6.0	2.5	3.0	25
FC-775	150	.01	8.9	22	8.5	400	1.5	59	11	.50	< 1.0	31
FC-797	19	.01	6.6	12	8.2	210	0.71	29	11	.30	< 1.0	14
FC-819	87	.01	12	15	8.4	550	1.6	71	12	.30	< 1.0	33
FC-836	76	.02	26	11	4.7	750	1.8	61	7.3	.20	< 1.0	.60
FC-853	240	.03	8.7	100	3.7	410	0.77	29	5.9	.30	< 1.0	.09

Site ID	Strontium, total (ppm)	Sulfur, total (%)	Tellurium, total (ppm)	Thallium, total (ppm)	Thorium, total (ppm)	Tin, total (ppm)	Titanium, total (%)	Tungsten, total (ppm)	Uranium, total (ppm)	Vanadium, total (ppm)	Yttrium, total (ppm)	Zinc, total (ppm)
FC-318	120	0.65	< 0.10	2.0	6.7	1.5	0.18	0.90	260	67	18	530
FC-324	89	.74	< .10	0.80	4.7	0.80	.11	.80	230	45	8.7	380
FC-334	100	1.0	< .10	2.9	7.8	1.0	.14	.80	61	54	7.9	22
FC-343	290	.44	< .10	1.8	17	1.9	.22	1.6	18	72	14	57
FC-355	91	.65	< .10	1.4	5.5	0.90	.15	.70	100	59	9.1	73
FC-697	82	.12	< .10	0.60	3.0	0.60	.08	2.2	160	38	6.6	49
FC-721	430	1.1	< .10	2.8	11	1.9	.25	1.2	520	110	32	160
FC-765	64	.35	< .10	1.1	4.3	0.70	.09	1.1	6.0	41	10	150
FC-771	100	.77	< .10	1.5	9.3	1.9	.21	2.3	210	82	20	200
FC-772	170	1.5	< .10	1.3	5.6	0.80	.14	.70	240	58	22	230
FC-775	140	.67	< .10	1.7	9.7	1.8	.23	1.0	240	80	15	99
FC-797	92	.37	< .10	0.90	9.9	1.4	.21	1.1	63	92	26	23
FC-819	120	.70	< .10	1.7	9.0	1.9	.18	1.2	350	87	17	64
FC-836	83	.85	< .10	1.3	6.5	0.90	.14	.70	370	73	27	50
FC-853	150	2.4	< .10	10	5.0	1.6	.08	.50	46	46	16	280

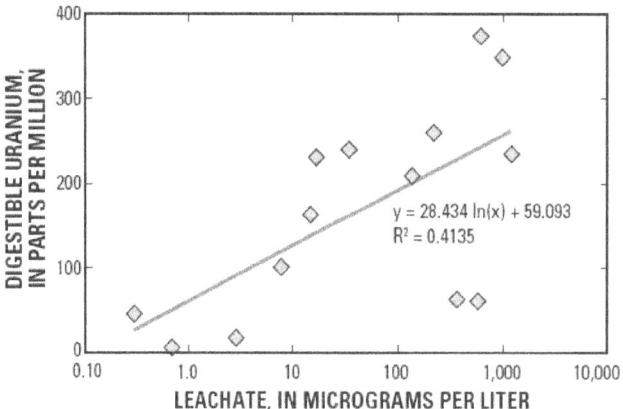

Figure 20. Relation between leachate and total digestible concentrations for uranium waste dump samples, Red, White, and Fry Canyons, southeastern Utah, 2007.

Table 7. Total extractible uranium concentration calculated from leachate concentration from uranium waste dump samples, Red, White, and Fry Canyons, southeastern Utah, 2007.

[Samples were analyzed at the U.S. Geological Survey Geologic Discipline Laboratory, Denver, Colorado. Site ID, site identification; MDT, Mountain Daylight Time; DD.dddd, Degrees.decimal degrees; ug/L, micrograms per liter; ppm, parts per million; FC, Fry Canyon area]

Site ID	Sample extraction date	Time (MDT)	Latitude (DD.dddd)	Longitude (DD.dddd)	Altitude (feet)	Uranium, dissolved (µg/L)	Uranium, total (ppm) calculated
FC-305	9/19/2007	1320	37.6302	110.16847	5,820	17	139
FC-314	9/19/2007	1340	37.65202	110.1831	5,860	0.65	47
FC-341	9/21/2007	1205	37.63183	110.1079	6,280	73	181
FC-348	9/20/2007	1230	37.63253	110.10883	6,280	29	155
FC-351	9/20/2007	1210	37.63408	110.11718	6,180	65	178
FC-394	9/21/2007	1120	37.56295	110 1024	6,200	46	168
FC-678	9/21/2007	1055	37.75673	110 2982	5,120	18	141
FC-687	9/19/2007	1445	37.67682	110 13437	6,240	42	165
FC-698	9/17/2007	1430	37.72662	110 20078	5,720	2.4	84
FC-702	9/21/2007	1200	37.70107	110 31898	4,600	4.0	98
FC-709	9/21/2007	1210	37.70945	110 3116	4,740	250	216
FC-710	9/17/2007	1440	37.73473	110 34942	4,520	1.5	70
FC-716	9/20/2007	1140	37.69552	110 32375	4,600	1.4	68
FC-725	9/17/2007	1425	37.72652	110 19988	5,760	40	164
FC-727	9/17/2007	1420	37.72618	110.19722	5,800	64	177
FC-735	9/17/2007	1500	37.54135	110.29038	4,820	1.7	73
FC-736	9/19/2007	1405	37.54418	110.29027	4,820	3.0	90
FC-748	9/19/2007	1455	37.54079	110.28602	4,840	18	142
FC-758	9/19/2007	1430	37.55754	110.29674	4,800	90	187
FC-767	9/20/2007	1150	37.57825	110 24085	5,360	1.3	67
FC-784	9/19/2007	1410	37.5693	110 23653	5,280	350	226
FC-791	9/19/2007	1345	37.58252	110 22608	5,400	11	126
FC-800	9/19/2007	1355	37.57296	110 20635	5,440	200	209
FC-814	9/20/2007	1300	37.57625	110 18958	5,720	140	199
FC-820	9/21/2007	1050	37.59627	110 19628	5,640	150	201
FC-828	9/21/2007	1150	37.60802	110 34152	4,360	0.73	50
FC-840	9/20/2007	1220	37.5846	110 12691	6,000	9.3	122
FC-857	9/17/2007	1450	37.54968	110 30207	4,800	8.0	118
FC-866	9/19/2007	1440	37.5492	110 30237	4,760	3.3	93
FC-885	9/19/2007	1335	37.5879	110 12867	5,980	8.8	121

area background samples. The waste rock sites do not support significant plant life and have an average leachate uranium concentration of 131 µg/L, while adjacent areas to the piles with significant plant life and potential for livestock forage have an average leachate uranium concentration of 7.6 µg/L. Because the natural background for the area is approximately 5 percent of the average uranium concentration found in the waste rock piles, radionuclide propagation by local plant life uptake was not considered.

Concentrations of uranium were converted to activity of uranium-238, as this is the most abundant naturally occurring isotope: 99.27 percent of natural uranium is uranium-238. Natural uranium consists of uranium-234, -235, and -238 in ratios corresponding to natural isotopic abundances which are less than 0.01 percent, 0.72 percent, and 99.27 percent, respectively. The uranium decay series considered includes the decay chain of uranium-238 to thorium-230. Radium-226 and its associated short-lived decay chain were considered as a separate radionuclide series. Given the three exposure pathways considered, radium-226 and its associated decay chain poses the greatest risk to human health shown by the model's sensitivity to radium-226 concentrations.

Due to the particular use in the area, some of the assumptions about the parameters used by RESRAD have been altered to fit the site conditions. The primary use of the area appears to be recreational, off-road activity by riders of all-terrain vehicles (ATV). Two primary use scenarios were considered in determining the amount of annual exposure a visitor experiences. The first scenario considered the duration of activities of an individual that lives near the area and visits the site periodically during any given year. The total annual visitation by an individual to the site was 4.6 days per year based on calculations made for daily duration of outdoor activities by a young adult (U.S. Environmental Protection Agency, 1997b, table 15.3). The second scenario considered the duration of time spent on the site by an individual who is using the area as a recreation destination and spends 7 to 14 days on the site, the latter equal to the maximum annual recreational occupancy of a site by the BLM. In all scenarios, RESRAD was setup to inspect three exposure pathways appropriate to the usage scenarios that were identified: (a) external gamma exposure, (b) inhalation exposure, and (c) soil ingestion exposure.

Modifications to default data used by RESRAD to calculate an annual radiation dosage were made in the "Occupancy" and "Ingestion: Dietary" subsections of modifiable data; in all other subsections, default data was used (Yu and others, 1993). In the "Occupancy" subsection, an inhalation rate of 14,016 m^3/year was used instead of the default of 8,400 m^3/year to reflect moderate activities by an individual either riding an ATV or involved in outdoor activities (U.S. Environmental Protection Agency, 1997b, table 5.23). The mass loading for inhalation was set to 0.0004 g/m^3 over the default 0.0001 g/m^3 to reflect the increased dust present on unpaved roads while ATV's are in use (Yu and others, 1993, chap. 35). The indoor time fraction was set to 0.0 instead of the default of 0.5,

inplying that the individual spends their entire time on the site outdoors. The outdoor time fraction was set appropriate to the annual exposure duration that was being considered: 0.013 for 4.6 days per year, 0.019 for 7.0 days per year, and 0.038 for 14.0 days per year. Outdoor time fractions are expressed as fractions of a one year period. In the "Ingestion: Dietary" subsection, a soil ingestion rate of 73 g/year was used instead of the default of 36.5 g/year to represent an average rate for all human age groups (U.S. Environmental Protection Agency, 1997b, table 4.23).

The resulting soil screening levels for combined uranium and radium for a maximum radiation dosage of 15 mrem/year are 96 pCi/g radium for 4.6 days per year, 66 pCi/g radium for 7.0 days per year, and 33 pCi/g radium for 14.0 days per year. At radium-uranium secular equilibrium, three sites, FC-721, FC-819, and FC-836, exceeded the 4.6 days-per-year SSL for radium. Ten additional sites, FC-318, FC-324, FC-709, FC-771, FC-772, FC-775, FC-784, FC-800, FC-814, and FC-820, exceeded the 7.0 days-per-year SSL for a total of thirteen sites. Eighteen additional sites, FC-305, FC-341, FC-348, FC-351, FC-355, FC-394, FC-678, FC-687, FC-697, FC-702, FC-725, FC-727, FC-748, FC-758, FC-791, FC-840, FC-857, and FC-885, exceeded the 14.0 days-per-year SSL for a total of 31 sites. At a radium-uranium activity ratio of 0.57, one site, FC-721, exceeded the 4.6 days-per-year SSL for radium. Two additional sites, FC-819 and FC-836, exceeded the 7.0 days-per-year SSL for a total of three sites. Fourteen additional sites, FC-318, FC-324, FC-341, FC-351, FC-709, FC-727, FC-758, FC-771, FC-772, FC-775, FC-784, FC-800, FC-814, and FC-820, exceeded the 14.0 days-per-year SSL for a total of fifteen sites (table 8).

Two assumptions were made when calculating the SSL values using RESRAD. One was that radium and uranium were at secular equilibrium, the other that the radium-uranium activity ratio was 0.57. When secular equilibrium was assumed, 31 sites exceeded a SSL and the majority, 16, were located in Red Canyon. At a radium-uranium activity ratio of 0.57, 17 sites exceeded a SSL and the majority, 12, were also located in Red Canyon. None of the sites located on Map 5 exceeded the calculated SSLs (fig. 6).

Future Work

Many uranium waste dumps in Red, White, and Fry Canyons contain elevated concentrations of trace elements as indicated from results of leachate analyses. On the basis of factors that include elevated leachate concentrations, basin drainage area, slope, and soil screening level exceedance, the following sites should be investigated further to assess potential risks to human health and the surrounding ecosystem: FC-318, FC-341, FC-351, FC-355, FC-394, FC-702, FC-709, FC-721, FC-727, FC-758, FC-771, FC-772, FC-775, FC-784, FC-800, FC-814, FC-819, FC-820, and FC-836.

Table 8. Radium concentrations calculated from total extractible uranium concentrations from uranium waste dump samples, Red, White and Fry Canyons, southeastern Utah, 2007.

[Samples were analyzed at the U S Geological Survey Geologic Discipline Laboratory, Denver, Colorado Site ID, site identification; MDT, Mountain Daylight Time; DD dddd, Degrees decimal degrees; ppm, parts per million; %, percent; pCi/g, picocuries per gram; FC, Fry Canyon area]

Site ID	Sample extraction date	Time (MDT)	Latitude (DD.dddd)	Longitude (DD.dddd)	Altitude (feet)	Uranium, total (ppm)	Uranium, as U-238 (pCi/g)	Radium, at 100% of U (pCi/g)	Radium, at 57% of U (pCi/g)
FC-318	9/21/2007	1045	37.66235	110.1984	5,660	260	87.5	87.5	49.9
FC-324	9/21/2007	1140	37.63702	110.11743	6,140	230	77.4	77.4	44.1
FC-334	9/20/2007	1240	37.6311	110.11207	6,220	61	20.5	20.5	11.7
FC-343	9/20/2007	1155	37.62942	110.10252	6,360	18	6.1	6.1	3.5
FC-355	9/20/2007	1225	37.6337	110.1177	6,100	100	33.7	33.7	19.2
FC-697	9/17/2007	1445	37.67545	110.22558	5,280	160	53.9	53.9	30.7
FC-721	9/19/2007	1435	37.55278	110.28272	4,880	520	175.1	175.1	99.8
FC-765	9/21/2007	1105	37.60642	110.33933	4,400	6	2.0	2.0	1.2
FC-771	9/19/2007	1415	37.5788	110.23853	5,280	210	70.7	70.7	40.3
FC-772	9/20/2007	1245	37.57905	110.2387	5,280	240	80.8	80.8	46.1
FC-775	9/20/2007	1145	37.57822	110.24068	5,360	240	80.8	80.8	46.1
FC-797	9/21/2007	1155	37.5814	110.20973	5,460	63	21.2	21.2	12.1
FC-819	9/19/2007	1450	37.5975	110.19318	5,680	350	117.8	117.8	67.2
FC-836	9/21/2007	1110	37.58912	110.15163	5,920	370	124.6	124.6	71.0
FC-853	9/21/2007	1040	37.76457	110.36922	4,280	46	15.5	15.5	8.8
Uranium concentrations below were calculated from regression equation									
FC-305	9/19/2007	1320	37.6302	110.16847	5,820	139	46.8	46.8	26.7
FC-314	9/19/2007	1340	37.65202	110.1831	5,860	47	15.8	15.8	9.0
FC-341	9/21/2007	1205	37.63183	110.1079	6,280	181	60.9	60.9	34.7
FC-348	9/20/2007	1230	37.63253	110.10883	6,280	155	52.2	52.2	29.7
FC-351	9/20/2007	1210	37.63408	110.11718	6,180	178	59.9	59.9	34.2
FC-394	9/21/2007	1120	37.56295	110.1024	6,200	168	56.6	56.6	32.2
FC-678	9/21/2007	1055	37.75673	110.2982	5,120	141	47.5	47.5	27.1
FC-687	9/19/2007	1445	37.67682	110.13437	6,240	165	55.6	55.6	31.7
FC-698	9/17/2007	1430	37.72662	110.20078	5,720	84	28.3	28.3	16.1
FC-702	9/21/2007	1200	37.70107	110.31898	4,600	98	33.0	33.0	18.8
FC-709	9/21/2007	1210	37.70945	110.3116	4,740	216	72.7	72.7	41.5
FC-710	9/17/2007	1440	37.73473	110.34942	4,520	70	23.6	23.6	13.4
FC-716	9/20/2007	1140	37.69552	110.32375	4,600	68	22.9	22.9	13.1
FC-725	9/17/2007	1425	37.72652	110.19988	5,760	164	55.2	55.2	31.5
FC-727	9/17/2007	1420	37.72618	110.19722	5,800	177	59.6	59.6	34.0
FC-735	9/17/2007	1500	37.54135	110.29038	4,820	73	24.6	24.6	14.0
FC-736	9/19/2007	1405	37.54418	110.29027	4,820	90	30.3	30.3	17.3
FC-748	9/19/2007	1455	37.54079	110.28602	4,840	142	47.8	47.8	27.3
FC-758	9/19/2007	1430	37.55754	110.29674	4,800	187	63.0	63.0	35.9
FC-767	9/20/2007	1150	37.57825	110.24085	5,360	67	22.6	22.6	12.9
FC-784	9/19/2007	1410	37.5693	110.23653	5,280	226	76.1	76.1	43.4
FC-791	9/19/2007	1345	37.58252	110.22608	5,400	126	42.4	42.4	24.2
FC-800	9/19/2007	1355	37.57296	110.20635	5,440	209	70.4	70.4	40.1
FC-814	9/20/2007	1300	37.57625	110.18958	5,720	199	67.0	67.0	38.2
FC-820	9/21/2007	1050	37.59627	110.19628	5,640	201	67.7	67.7	38.6
FC-828	9/21/2007	1150	37.60802	110.34152	4,360	50	16.8	16.8	9.6
FC-840	9/20/2007	1220	37.5846	110.12691	6,000	122	41.1	41.1	23.4
FC-857	9/17/2007	1450	37.54968	110.30207	4,800	118	39.7	39.7	22.6
FC-866	9/19/2007	1440	37.5492	110.30237	4,760	93	31.3	31.3	17.8
FC-885	9/19/2007	1335	37.5879	110.12867	5,980	121	40.7	40.7	23.2

References Cited

Briggs, P.H., 2002, The determination of forty elements in geological and botanical samples by inductively coupled plasma-atomic emission spectrometry, *in* Taggart, J.E., Jr., ed., Analytical methods for chemical analysis of geologic and other materials: U.S. Geological Survey Open-File Report 02-223-G, p. G1–G18.

Brown, Z.A., O'Leary, R.M., Hageman, P.L., and Crock, J.G., 2002, Mercury in water, geologic, and plant materials by continuous flow-cold vapor-atomic absorption spectrometry, *in* Taggart, J.E., Jr., ed., Analytical methods for chemical analysis of geologic and other materials: U.S. Geological Survey Open-File Report 02-223-M, p. M1–M9.

Crock, J.G., Lichte, F.E., and Briggs, P.H., 1983, Determination of elements in National Bureau of Standards geological reference materials SRM 278 obsidian and SRM 688 basalt by inductively coupled plasma-atomic emission spectroscopy: Geostandards Newsletter, v. 7, no. 2, p. 335–340.

Hageman, P.L., and Briggs, P.H., 2000, A simple field leach test for rapid screening and qualitative characterization of mine uranium waste dump material on abandoned mine lands: Proceedings from the Fifth International Conference on Acid Rock Drainage, Denver, Colorado, May 21–24, 2000, p. 1463-1475.

Hageman, P.L., Brown, Z.A., and Welsch, E., 2002, Arsenic and selenium by flow injection or continuous flow-hydride generation-atomic absorption spectrophotometry, *in* Taggart, J.E., Jr., ed., Analytical methods for chemical analysis of geologic and other materials: U.S. Geological Survey Open-File Report 02-223-L, p. L1–L7.

Hintze, L.F., Willis, G.C., Laes, D.Y.M., Sprinkle, D.A., and Brown, K.D., 1996, Digital compilation of geologic map of Utah: U.S. Geological Survey Digital Data Series 41.

Kenney, T.A., Wilkowske, C.D., and Wright, S.J., 2007, Methods for estimating magnitude and frequency of peak flows for natural streams in Utah: U.S. Geological Survey Scientific Investigations Report 2007-5158, 28 p.

Natural Resources Conservation Service, 1998, Utah Annual Precipitation [map], scale: 1:1,000,000, Source 1008501.

Ries, K.G., III, Steeves, P.A., Coles, J.D., Rea, A.H., and Stewart, D.W., 2004, StreamStats: A U.S. Geological Survey web application for stream information: U.S. Geological Survey Fact Sheet 2004-3115.

Smith, K.S., Ramsey, C.A., and Hageman, P.L., 2000, Sampling strategy for the rapid screening of mine-waste dumps on abandoned mine lands: Proceedings from the Fifth International Conference on Acid Rock Drainage, Denver, Colorado, May 21–24, 2000, p. 1453–1461.

Stearn, T.W., and Stieff, L.R., 1959, Geochemistry and mineralogy of the Colorado Plateau uranium ores: Part 13. Radium-uranium equilibrium and radium-uranium ages of some secondary minerals, U.S. Geological Survey Professional Paper 320, 1959. p. 151–156.

U.S. Environmental Protection Agency, 1997a, Memorandum —Establishment of cleanup levels for CERCLA sites with radioactive contamination. OSWER No. 9200.4-18. Washington, DC, August 1997.

U.S. Environmental Protection Agency, 1997b, Exposure factors handbook. Washington, DC, EPA/600/P-95/002F a-c, 1997.

U.S. Environmental Protection Agency, 2007a, Current national recommended water quality criteria for aquatic life: U.S. Environmental Protection Agency database, accessed January 21, 2007, at *http://www.epa.gov/waterscience/criteria/wqcriteria.html*.

U.S. Environmental Protection Agency, 2007b, Drinking water contaminants: U.S. Environmental Protection Agency database, accessed January 22, 2007, at *http://www.epa.gov/safewater/contaminants/index.html*.

Wilde, F.D., ed., 2004, Cleaning of equipment for water sampling (ver. 2.0): U.S. Geological Survey Techniques of Water-Resources Investigations, book 9, chap. A3, accessed October 10, 2006, at *http://pubs.water.usgs.gov/twri9A3/*.

Yu, C., Loureiro, C., Cheng, J.J., Jones, L.G., Wang, Y.Y., Chia, Y.P., and Faillance, E., 1993, Data collection handbook to support modeling impacts of radioactive material in soil. Environmental Assessment and Information Sciences Division, Argonne National Laboratory, Argonne, Illinois, 1993.

Appendix A. Chemical Analysis of Leachate Samples from Uranium Waste Dump Sites, Background Sites, and Streambed Sediment Sites, for Major-Ion and Trace-Element Concentrations, Red, White, and Fry Canyons, Southeastern Utah, 2007.

Appendix A is a Microsoft Excel spreadsheet, a separate, associated document from this report. This table is titled, *Chemical analysis of leachate samples from uranium waste dump sites, background sites, and streambed sediment sites, for major-ion and trace-element concentrations, Red, White, and Fry Canyons, southeastern Utah, 2007*. This table is available online and is recommended to be downloaded with the main report, Scientific Investigations Report 2010-5108. Place this Excel document on the same file level as the main report. This will enable any links associated with the document to function between the main report and the Excel file.